Flavors of Faith: Holy Breads

How the simplest combination of
flour, water and yeast becomes
a spiritual cornerstone of
family, faith and community

Lynne Meredith Golodner

D0104669

Read The Spirit Books
an imprint of
David Crumm Media, LLC
Canton, Michigan

For more information and further discussion, visit
www.TheFlavorsOfFaith.com

Follow the author at www.LynneGolodner.com

Cover art and design by
Rick Nease
www.RickNeaseArt.com

Photo of bakers in the mosque by the author.
All other photos by Stephanie Fenton

Published By
Read The Spirit Books
an imprint of
David Crumm Media, LLC
42015 Ford Rd., Suite 234
Canton, Michigan, USA

For information about customized editions, bulk purchases
or permissions, contact David Crumm Media, LLC at info@
DavidCrummMedia.com

Contents

Dedication

To my children, Asher, Eliana, Grace and Shaya, who add meaning to every day and have opened my eyes to the beauty of life.

The best bread ... came from the kitchen of a very simple woman, who knew instinctively that she could solace her loneliness through the ritual of honest cooking. It taught me, although I did not understand it then, a prime lesson in survival [that] I must eat well. And in these days of spurious and distorted values, the best way to eat is simply, without affectation or adulteration. Given honest flour, pure water and a good fire, there is really only one more thing needed to make the best bread in the world, fit for the greatest gourmet ever born: and that is honest love.

—**American food writer M.F.K. Fisher (1908-1992)**

How To Use This Book
Organizing an Exciting Small Group

ENJOY EATING? FASCINATED with faith? Like to share with friends? Then, you're going to *love* this book and the series it is launching about the intersection of food and faith.

It is a universal cornerstone of faith traditions on the planet to nourish one another at times of celebration and of sadness. We commemorate our shared histories and communities through food. This series, *The Flavors of Faith*, will provide insight and inspiration from a variety of faith communities about how food can be symbol and ritual, significant and fun, in communicating our faith traditions.

This book is ideal for small group discussion. Groups like yours have been our audience from the outset; with a vision of coming together to learn, taste and savor the many ways we nurture spirituality through food. Millions of small groups meet in congregations, libraries, coffee shops and living rooms nationwide. Many small groups are called "Sunday school" or "Bible study." Colleagues who work together or stay-at-home moms often organize their own weekly groups. Men like to call their gatherings a "morning prayer group" or a "men's breakfast" while others are known as a "sisterhood" or "brotherhood." Groups vary widely in focus and format—but there is one nearly universal custom: food.

We all enjoy eating as we gather with friends. Thousands of inspirational books are designed for small-group discussions, especially for circles that meet in congregations. However, after years of research into new ways to help enliven these assemblies, we discovered one missing element: Few books published for such groups focus on our universal enjoyment of food. Millions gather. We thrive on true friendship. We talk. We eat. But almost no one tries to build an inspirational series around the food itself—nor understand the very roots of our food traditions.

Veteran food writer Lynne Meredith Golodner and ReadTheSpirit Books plan to change that with this first in a series we are calling *The Flavors of Faith*. This book focuses on the simplest food that expresses love for our families, our faith and our hospitality toward the world: bread. Nearly every religion and culture on Earth has an ancient tradition of sharing bread in this way.

In preparing *The Flavors of Faith*, we have talked with small group participants nationwide. People are hungry for this book. As you open these pages, you will want to convey that excitement to the people around you. Early in this book, you will enjoy a bread literally entwined with Christian tradition. The religious inspiration behind pretzels is believed to stretch back more than a millennium. To this day, pretzel history is celebrated in many parts of the world, especially in southern Pennsylvania's Amish country where visitors can tour one of this nation's oldest pretzel bakeries. In 2012, U.S. pretzel sales approached $1 billion. In short: You'll encounter familiar flavors and unusual breads in this book—as well as some sure-fire crowd pleasers like fresh-baked pretzels.

If you are a group leader, start by inviting a couple of friends to help you organize your weekly series using this book. You might invite them to discuss the idea with you and bring some fresh-baked pretzels to the planning meeting. You'll also want to flip through the book and choose participants who will have fun tackling the recipes in each of the chapters. Don't miss the final chapter in which participants will discover a Baby Jesus nestled in a festive cake. It's fun to think of tearing open a tasty, home-baked sweet bread and discovering—in one lucky piece—a tiny figure of Jesus. It also may be a little intimidating to first-time home cooks who have never encountered this custom or shopped for these little figurines. Consider showing up at your planning meeting with Baby Jesus figures all set for the series. You can find them easily on www.Amazon.com, many bakery supply stores or catalogs of housewares that many of us receive in the mail.

Why so much emphasis on Christianity in this book? The latest study of worldwide religious affiliation by the Pew Research Center shows 4 out of 5 Americans identifying as Christian; worldwide, Christians comprise 1 in 3 people living on planet Earth. The vast majority of small groups meeting each week across the United States are associated with churches. But—Pew research also shows that Americans are fascinated by other world faiths and cultural traditions. So, in these pages, you also will find chapters on Jewish, Muslim and Native American breads. In secular settings, cultural competency is now regarded as a valuable professional goal and this book is a terrific opportunity for schools, libraries and even work-based groups to learn about the cross-cultural traditions in our communities.

How should you organize the group? This depends on your setting. A community-wide group focusing on cross-cultural education may want to invite guest speakers from various religious and ethnic groups to visit each week and tell their own stories about these traditions. Or, a church-based Sunday school group might want to highlight the "Lord's Prayer" and encourage members to pray that central Christian prayer each day, reflecting on Jesus' words about daily bread in new ways. Choose your own pathway through this process of sharing stories and recipes. You'll have no problem with group members arriving late, if they know these treats are awaiting them!

Who bakes? We suggest that group members select chapters to prepare individually or in small teams, baking that week's bread for the entire group. Begin each group by enjoying that treat and the hospitality that flows with such a traditional action of breaking bread. Each chapter provides an inspiring and educational story about that week's recipe as a starting point—and group participants naturally will want to dig deeper. Encourage participants to make their own inquiries through family, friends, the larger community or even other world cultures. Invite participants to bring inspiring stories about food traditions they enjoy. Share fond family memories. Beyond the home, encourage participants to bring stories about their neighborhoods. In the book's first chapter, you will read Bill Tonelli's vivid story about a neighborhood bakery when he was growing up in South Philadelphia. Those local stories, coupled with the subsequent chapters in this book, will turn your weekly gatherings into can't-miss events.

Where are the discussion questions? Where are the Bible citations? Most books published for small groups include specific questions to ask participants; and most of these books designed for congregations include Bible verses. *The Flavors of Faith* is a different kind of small-group experience. Each week, volunteers in your group will arrive energized by having prepared the baked goods that everyone will share. They will have shopped for ingredients, baked the bread—and thought about how that week's chapter resonates in the lives of people they know. We have not included specific questions in this book, but you will have no shortage of spirited conversation that you can shape as most suitable to your community.

When should you start? Any time. Don't wait for a particular season. You may associate pretzels with Lent or king cake with Mardi Gras, depending on your own family history and region of the country, but the truth is: Today, these foods are enjoyed throughout the year. Even a custom as specific as king cake has multiple connections throughout the Christian calendar.

If you enjoy this book, please tell others! If you take any lesson from this series, it's a rediscovery of the power of nurturing and nourishing ourselves, and those around us; of sharing and hospitality. Beyond your own circle, we invite you to check out www.TheFlavorsOfFaith.com to find additional stories about faith and food. More than that, we invite you to share your own stories, recipes and tips with readers through our website. Got a question for us? Or, a question to ask other readers? There are opportunities on the website to connect, share and inquire.

Enjoy this adventure in faith, food and hospitality!

chapter 1

The Power in Our Daily Bread

Reclaiming the Staff of Life

Give us this day, our daily bread ...
  Got any dough?
  I'm outta bread, man.
  The bread, the body ...

SLANG FOR MONEY, a Divine symbol, a basic staple made from the commonest of ingredients, bread is both simple and profound. While politics and religion can tear people apart, bread brings people together. Shared by virtually every community, bread takes center stage at festive celebrations and on the most sacred of ritual tables. It's no wonder that many of the world's greatest prayers and blessings reflect on bread!

This cornerstone of faith and ritual is universal. Whether it is risen or flat, sweet or plain, bread and water are the minimum to sustain a prisoner and the crescendo of a High Mass. Bread springs from the deepest roots of civilization. More than 12,000 years ago, people made flat breads of flour and water, mixed and packed into dough that rose on a rock in the sun. The ancient Greeks claimed more than 50 kinds of bread. The Romans created the concept of a public bakery. The Christian Bible references bread hundreds of times. In America, the "breadwinner" is the person who supports the family. In Russia, one of the words for hospitality translates roughly to "bread and salt." Italian writer Bill Tonelli says the bread we are born into is the bread we eat.

A Neighborhood Defined by its Bread

Bill Tonelli doesn't know what propelled him to write his 2008 *Washington Post* essay, "Take This (Portuguese) Bread." Mostly an editor, Tonelli says it takes great pains to write something good, but this story of the bread of a community was so much a part of his South Philadelphia childhood, that he had pretty much written the entire piece in his head before he took pen to paper.

"The beauty of bread is that it's God and the devil all in one," Tonelli says. "It's flour and water, at minimum. It's pretty universally available and, nutritionally speaking, it is kind of the cheapest, worst food in the world—if you want to call it food. It's practically poison today, the whole idea of bread."

But, growing up in the Little Italy of Philadelphia, bread defined his sense of community, identity and weekly celebration. Every Sunday, Tonelli's grandmother and all the other grandmothers in the neighborhood would time their walk just right so that they would line up at the neighborhood bakery at the perfect moment when the bread was still warm and they could carry it home for the entire family to break open—steam rising forth—over the Sunday table.

At about 1 p.m. on Sundays in South Philly during the 1950s and 1960s, the streets were empty, Tonelli recalls. Everyone sat down around their tables and recited a non-descript, rote grace, tore open their bread and dredged it, piping hot, through the gravy on their macaroni. It was what they did after church—the way families came together.

"Each neighborhood had a bakery," says Tonelli, whose New York neighborhood today is more Portuguese than Italian, still with a bakery. There was a rhythm to living in those days: at 6 a.m., old Italian immigrant men walked to the bakery, flipped the lights on, fired up the ovens and began pounding away at the dough that would rise and lift to sustain the families who were their loyal customers. Later in the morning, the old Italian grandmothers, with their head scarves and long, full skirts, walked the same path to stand in line for the freshest bread.

Tonelli's bakery was called Inperiale's, the name of the family that owned it. "There wasn't anything such as competition in one neighborhood," he said. A neighborhood could sustain perhaps two bars or two groceries, but only one bakery—plain and simple.

"You had a church and a school and a playground and a bakery," he says. "It was as if each neighborhood was assigned one or grew up around one. It was part of your neighborhood. It was where you went. They were all pretty good."

They were more than good. The way Tonelli's neighbors and friends talk about their bakery carries with it a deep sense of pride, like they were "jewels" to treasure. "It was our bakery and that was our bread and without thinking about it, we expressed a loyalty to our bread the way we expressed loyalty to ourselves," says Tonelli.

Bread in hand, "the old ladies would close the top of the bag as tight as they could and clench it so the warmth would stay in the bread," he says. "If the timing was right, and you sat down to eat at 1 o'clock, those rolls were still warm inside. Most people went from church to the bakery on the way home, the route planned so the bread was as fresh as possible.

"We all kept the Italian tradition of the big meal of the day around 1 o'clock on Sundays as everybody I knew did," he says. "Sunday was the day of all the days of the week that was most important to have bread. We ate bread constantly."

As society has moved away from cherishing bread as the centerpiece of the family table, some elemental value of humanity has disappeared as well, Tonelli says. "When bread went away, it was something more than just bread that went away.

"I love bread," says Tonelli, who lived in Italy for a while and found himself rising early to bring home fresh warmth for his own children. "I understand the elemental power of bread. It's just a couple of ingredients and somehow it is: 'Give us this day our daily bread. ...' It's money. It's everything. I don't know where bread leaves off and we begin."

An Ancient Hunger: Needing and Kneading Bread

Colloquially, the words "bread" and "dough" are slang for money. And think about the cliché, "The greatest thing since sliced bread!" That familiar saying still equates something new and compelling with Americans' collective wonderment in the late 1920s when sliced loaves began appearing on grocery shelves.

In many languages, the word for bread is synonymous with the word for life, breath or other spiritually sustaining notions. In all branches of Christianity, bread is symbolic of God and in Catholic theology, bread actually becomes a piece of the Holy. In Judaism, there is a religious proscription to "take challah," where a piece of dough offering was set aside in biblical times to give to the holy priests in the Temple. In the days since the Temple's destruction, religious Jews burn a piece of dough beyond recognition to symbolize their inability to worship at the spiritual center in Jerusalem. The lengthiest prayers in Hebrew are those for meals that begin with bread.

Since ancient times, bread has been sacred—connected with rituals from fertility to the hope of resurrection. Since the Neolithic period, mythology and ritual have paralleled devotion to and dependence on plant life, because the mysterious beginnings and endings of human life mirror the lifecycle of plants.

Think about this: The definition of Bethlehem or *beit lechem,* a Hebrew word for one of the most significant biblical cities is, "house of bread." Throughout the Bible, God's generosity is displayed as sustenance, often in the form of bread. First, to the Israelites as they trudge through the desert, as daily gifts of manna. Scholars say that the significance of manna presages the Christian Eucharist, a sign of God's enduring generosity. In the Exodus story, when the Jews were wandering in the desert, six out of seven days in the week, manna arrived to nourish every person in the community. If Jews took more than their intended daily portion, the extra would rot. However, included in the Exodus story is the tradition that on Fridays, the day before the Jewish Sabbath, God gave each person a double portion of manna that would not spoil but would hold over so that they had sustenance on the Sabbath day, when no work was permitted. The implicit trust in God and sense of community that runs through the story of the manna is deep and indelible.

"I would argue that as many years as the Israelites were

wandering in the wilderness, there were people who were sick and people who gathered the manna for them," says Carter Echols, interim director of church relations for Bread for the World in Washington, D.C. "The promise is that everybody had enough."

Considering the entire sweep of the biblical narrative from Passover to manna to loaves and fishes to the Last Supper, Echols says, "Bread is a call to community. Around the table, we are called to be community together."

In the story of Jesus feeding a huge crowd with a tiny number of loaves and fishes, Echols believes that "the great miracle was that everybody had bread in their pockets and they were willing to share, and when they actually shared what they had, there was more than enough." That story echoes so many others, she says. "Twelve baskets for 12 tribes. Always it is about community. It's not about eating. Think of Abraham and Sarah, Elijah and the widow. It's about feeding each other. God has given us each other. Our scripture says where two or three are gathered together, Christ is there."

World religions often collide, but Echols says they share a common faith in "the value of hospitality, community" and the importance of feeding one another in body and soul.

Rediscovering the Health in Our Daily Bread

Have you watched people with bread in restaurants? Yoga moms tearing out the pulp in the middle of a bagel half to reduce the number of "carbs" they consume; young girls limiting their bread intake at fancy dinners because they've been taught that bread is bad; low carb, no carb, nothing white. We deprive ourselves for an unrealistic, unattainable goal—and in the process, we have lost the basic foundation of sustenance and spirituality.

Bread represents that what is basic is essential. Made up of mere ingredients that are attainable by the masses and magically transformed into something sustaining and nourishing, bread is a timeless food that, when nothing else is available, keeps people going.

As a longtime journalist and specialist in writing about food, such scenes sadden me. Our affluent society is in conflict with the staff of life. In contemporary culture, bread has become our enemy—a fat-producing, calorie-intensive food that we must ration and avoid. Bill Tonelli describes that as seeing the devil in our bread. However, as you explore this book and consider the long and vital history of bread's sustaining power, you will find that our avoidance of bread today is signaling a deeper and potentially unquenchable hunger. Even as we identify bread as a villain in the food stories we tell ourselves, we forget that bread represents salvation for billions of men and women.

This story is my story as much as it is yours. When I was new to a more faithful life, I marked my newfound observance through the ritual of bread baking. In my Jewish tradition, challah (you'll read about this in Chapter 3) launches every Sabbath meal and most holidays. In my childhood home and in so many homes, bread comes in a bag from the supermarket. As an adult raising my own family, I decided that the ability to bake our own bread was an independence that I needed to claim. If I could bake my own bread, I could be responsible for my own spirituality, my own observance, the nourishing of my growing family.

For years when my children were small, they stood on kitchen chairs and helped me knead the dough. They added ingredients to the standing mixer and peeked under the kitchen towel to see if the dough had risen. They shaped loaves in pretty much every form they could muster and proudly claimed their finished product once the loaves had cooled on a wire rack beside the oven. At our Sabbath table, each child proudly palmed their handmade challah, knowing from a young age that they were responsible for creating their own spiritual significance.

I have always been concerned about the roots of my family's food. I go to great lengths to buy local food, recently harvested, from farmers' markets, even in my cold Michigan climate. We buy milk from a local farm and when we eat meat, we make sure it is devoid of antibiotics, hormones and chemicals that might wreak havoc on our fragile systems.

We make food from scratch and gather around the family table to share in life together. With four ravenous, growing children, my husband and I realized recently that we consume a lot of bread. Sandwiches, toast, French toast—there are so many ways my children consume bread that we got to a point where even two loaves a week went far quicker than we anticipated.

So we decided to make our own bread. We started with Mark Bittman's *How to Cook Everything* (my kitchen bible!) and made a sourdough starter, which we left to ferment in the kitchen for two days. When it was sufficiently sour, we followed the recipe and made a hearty loaf of sourdough so delicious, it was consumed by our family faster than any store-bought loaf. The great thing about sourdough or any bread with a starter is that you use half and replenish the starter, so you are ready to make a new batch virtually all the time.

We went on with this recipe for weeks, each batch a different lightness or flavor than the week prior. In my kitchen, I have a collection of cookbooks representing our travels, our traditions and the foods we prefer. Among them are several bread cookbooks. We have dog-eared pages to remember the loaves we'd like to try.

The way I bake bread, it is a two-person endeavor, at least. Don't worry, no recipe requires that—but it is the art of building something and fostering even a small family community that draws me to this. I wouldn't necessarily make a loaf of bread just to nourish myself. As so many traditions say, where two or more gather, God dwells, and I believe that is inherent in the food we make. When we prepare food for others, we are inviting the Divine to dwell among us. When we care enough to devote time and attention to the details of creating something raised from something inconsequential and barely noticed, we are emulating God.

When my husband travels for work, I don't have time or energy to bake bread. In those rare weeks, we resort to store-bought loaves, and we all notice the difference. There is something so special about the scent of home-baked bread filling a home. My children grab slices as soon as they are cool enough to touch. They don't need butter or jelly or any topping—it is tasty enough and soul-satisfying as it is.

When I bake bread, I believe I am connecting with all those who came before me in this essential endeavor. We are united; we share a tradition, a lineage, which is so much more than food. And it is these types of traditions that I am most proud to pass along to my children. For the rest of their lives, when they taste a bread we made in our home, they will recall a simpler time, a time filled with love, a time when they knew they were loved and cared for and part of something so big.

This is both a spiritual matter and a matter of public health. The 2012 Global Hunger Index reports 57 countries around the world face serious issues with hunger, but the most alarming news in this latest Hunger Index is that global efforts to combat hunger are slowing in the midst of stressed economies across the developed world. Daily bread is the hope of life for men, women and children around the world. Yet, we have become strangely ambivalent toward this life-sustaining food.

Throughout history, bread has been life's foundation. The

rise of civilization in Africa and the Middle East was associated with the cultivation of more robust varieties of grain and the resulting breads that sustained entire villages, then entire nations. Historic eras of injustice and transformation often turned on the availability and cost of bread. Symbols of bread connect with procreation, fertility, family life, a thriving economy and spiritual elevation. Bread is intimate. The making of bread is sensual, almost an erotic act. The further we stray from the origins of this most elemental food, I fear, the further we stray from our own ability to be comfortable in our selves, to connect with others and to find real friendship and intimacy.

Reclaiming Bread as Sacrament

"Give us this day our daily bread." More than 2 billion Christians around the world are instructed to raise that prayer.

"Food is so ordinary that we overlook it as we make grand quests for spiritual understanding and enlightenment. Yet the religions of the world have understood its profound significance, its luscious imagery, and its weight in meaning," writes Thomas Moore, in *The Interiority of Food.*

Christians of nearly all denominations define a sacrament as a religious action in which God is uniquely active. Catholics and Protestants vary on further details of that definition, including how many ritual acts qualify as sacraments. But, there is no escaping Jesus' central focus on bread in his ministry as recorded in the Gospels. In fact, much of Jesus' public works can be described as "meal ministry," says Father Dan Merz, associate director of The Committee on Divine Worship for the United States Conference of Catholic Bishops. Father Merz's conclusion echoes readings of the Gospels by many contemporary Bible scholars.

Most popular are stories of Jesus' supernatural ability to multiply food for crowds. When reading or hearing those stories today, Father Merz urges readers to focus on the extraordinarily nourishing quality of what Jesus provides. Jesus was Jewish and knew the importance of the Exodus, the manna in the desert and the sustaining power of God embodied in bread. To this day, the very presence of bread is a symbol of God's nurture—and bread's exquisite and satisfying flavor reminds us of the reward for ultimate faith in the Divine, Father Merz says.

For nearly 2,000 years, Christian leaders and secular Bible scholars have debated the unusual Greek word *epiousios*, translated as "daily" in "Give us this day our daily bread." Catholic tradition, in particular, connects this word to the centrality of bread in the Eucharist becoming Christ, sufficient to nourish our souls. Father Merz says the word underlines that Jesus was referring to bread not as a complete, physical meal. "It was never intended as a full, physically satisfying meal," he says, "but rather as one that satisfies our deeper needs and desires." The goal in celebrating the Mass is communing with God in the act of eating and, thus, elevating our lives.

Beliefs about what happens to the bread during communion were at the heart of the Protestant division within Christianity half a millennium ago. Protestants regard the bread more as a symbolic reminder of Jesus. Nevertheless, all Christians around the world teach that fellowship around a shared table does more for our souls than quickly eating alone to sustain our bodies.

"We are not animals, but children of God with a soul," says Father Merz. "We do indeed eat in order to live, just as the animals do, but by the fact that we have a soul, we have the possibility of raising mere eating for physical sustenance into dining for spiritual and social well-being. *Koinonia,* or communion, is an effect of the energy of the Holy Spirit, who reaches out to our spirit through this *epiousios* bread that we receive in the Eucharist. This bread bonds those who sit around the table of the altar together in *koinonia* with the Holy Spirit."

Other traditions share this reverence for bread and food as a hallmark of our faith. In Jewish tradition, there is a specific blessing to recite before taking a first bite and then a succession of prayers after a meal finishes. The idea behind these recitations is that we elevate ourselves above the animals by making the act of eating—a necessity, if we are to live and be well—something meaningful and God-given. With every bite, we remember what we believe and who we are, why we are here and where our food comes from.

From formal theology to the most universal spiritual truths, the sacred story of bread is the elevation of one of life's simplest cornerstones by experience, by tradition, by prayer into something that gives lives around the world transcendent meaning.

Emily Dickinson (1830-1886) knew that truth. She is famous, today, for her reclusive life and her exquisite poetry, crafted in the privacy of her home. Her first collection of verse wasn't published until after her death. Yet, Dickinson publicly prided herself on one skill: baking bread. In her 20s, she developed this talent and became well known among her neighbors for producing several kinds of bread. She even claimed a prize for one of her loaves at an 1856 Amherst, Massachusetts fair.

Only one year before winning that prize, she had written to a friend, "I am going to learn to make bread tomorrow. So you may imagine me with my sleeves rolled up, mixing flour, milk, etc., with a great deal of grace. I advise you—if you don't know how to make the staff of life—to learn with dispatch."

Emily Dickinson's Coconut Cake

Makes one 9-by-5-inch loaf. Emily Dickinson was an accomplished baker and did not provide any instructions in her hand-written version. She wrote the ingredients in pencil on the back of one of her poems and also noted that she had borrowed

this "cocoanut" cake recipe from Mrs. Carmichael, a neighbor in Amherst. Various modern cooks have pieced together the directions. This is a simple quick bread or cake, although it was not overly sweet. **Note:** Baking soda plus cream of tartar equals baking powder. Most home cooks today will want to substitute 1½ teaspoons baking powder for the soda and cream of tartar. Emily made her own compound by combining soda and cream of tartar. If you use common sweetened Baker's coconut, which wasn't commercially available in Emily's era, it will sweeten the cake.

2 cups all-purpose flour (To lighten the cake, you may substitute 2 cups plus 2 tablespoons cake flour.)
1½ teaspoons baking powder (substitution for ½ teaspoon baking soda plus
  1 teaspoon cream of tartar)
1 cup sugar
1 stick (½ cup) butter, softened
2 eggs
½ cup milk

1 cup grated coconut
(If using dried, soak in warm water until soft and drain
well before adding to the batter; or use soft, sweetened
Baker's coconut.)

Preheat oven to 350°F. Butter or oil a 9-by-5-inch loaf
pan; set aside. In a medium bowl, combine flour and
baking powder; set aside.

In a large bowl of an electric mixer, blend sugar and
butter until light and fluffy. Add the eggs, and then mix
in the milk.

Add the flour mixture and beat until just combined.
Fold in the coconut. Spread the batter into the prepared loaf pan. Check after 35 minutes, testing with
a toothpick. Baking time may vary. Bake until golden
brown and toothpick comes out clean.

* * *

If you'd like to try your hand at a simple, every day bread
as discussed in this chapter, here is an easy and delicious
recipe from Detroit-based food writer and chef, Annabel
Cohen.

Easy Rosemary Garlic Peasant Bread

Makes 1 round loaf.
Some years ago, my friend Annabel Cohen offered up a version of this recipe she found in the New York Times. I "married" her recipe to another one I found on a cooking website. Both recipes were billed as "no knead" so they're quite easy to prepare. The recipe always comes out

perfect. My version of this bread includes rosemary and fresh garlic, but you can easily leave them out for a rustic white bread. **Note:** This dough must rest overnight.

3 cups bread flour
¼ teaspoon instant yeast (not active dry yeast)
1½ teaspoons kosher salt
1½ cups water, room temperature
3 tablespoons fresh rosemary leaves
1 tablespoons fresh chopped garlic
Cornmeal, for crust
Olive oil, for plastic wrap and pot

In a large bowl combine flour, yeast, and salt. Add the water, rosemary leaves and garlic and stir until blended—dough will be sticky. Cover bowl with plastic wrap. Let dough rest 18 or more hours at room temperature. The dough will become bubbly.

Remove the dough to a generously floured surface and fold the dough over itself twice. With the dough still on the floured surface, cover with oiled plastic wrap. Allow the dough to rest for 15 minutes.

Remove the plastic wrap. Using floured hands, form the dough into a ball.

Place a clean cotton dishtowel (not terry cloth) on a clean, dry surface. Sprinkle about ½ cup cornmeal on the towel. Roll the dough ball in the cornmeal to cover (add more cornmeal, if desired), and place another clean towel over the dough ball. Allow the dough to rise for 2 hours. The ball will double in size.

Preheat oven to 425°F. Heat a 6-quart ovenproof pot with a lid (usually stainless steel, enamel, cast iron or a Dutch oven) in the oven for 30 minutes.

Remove pot from oven, carefully oil it and place the dough ball in the hot pot. Cover and bake for 30 minutes. Reduce the oven temperature to 375°F, remove the lid and continue baking for 30-40 minutes, until the crust is browned. Cool the bread before running a knife around the pot to turn out the loaf.

—My friend Annabel Cohen is a writer, chef and food stylist. She continues to be a featured expert on subjects culinary and lifestyle on television and radio programs and can often be seen cooking on local weekend news shows. She was selected by *Crain's Detroit Business* as a one of the city's most passionate cooks. Annabel was featured as "Detroit's Ultimate Food Writer" on the Travel Channel's *Food Wars* and was the deciding judge comparing two Detroit landmarks: Lafayette Coney Island and American Coney Island. Fluent in Spanish and Portuguese and hailing from a Brazilian-Jewish family, Annabel travels the world, expanding her cooking repertoire. Annabel co-authored *Eating for Acid Reflux; a Handbook and Cookbook for Those with Heartburn* (2003), and *America's Thanksgiving Parade Cookbook* (1998), a cookbook celebrating and benefiting this popular national event. Annabel also supplied the recipe for maple pecan-topped cornbread in chapter 4, "Native American Breads."

chapter 2

Arms Crossed in Prayer

The Holy Origins of Pretzels

A **FAVORITE SNACK** food of toddlers and an easy-dipping rod for college parties, the pretzel actually springs from religion. Pretzels are a simple food, made of simple ingredients: flour, yeast and water. Some include salt. These ingredients were approved for the Lenten fasting period centuries ago, making the pretzel a staple food during that time. That was an era when Western Christians took the Lenten fast more seriously. (Eastern Christians maintain that fast to this day.) In Western Christian fasting, the church mandated only one meal a day along with small bites and bits—like a pretzel—to maintain strength throughout the day, according to Father William Saunders, dean of the Notre Dame Graduate School of Christendom College and pastor of Our Lady of Hope Parish in Sterling, Virginia. "A need arose for a very simple food which would fulfill the abstinence and fasting laws," wrote Saunders in a 2003 article entitled "Lenten Pretzels."

There are other stories of this crispy snack bread's origins, though. One legend has it that an Italian monk in the early 600s prepared a special Lenten bread made of water, flour and salt. He rolled the dough in strips, and then crossed the strips as if to form them into a representation of crossed arms (which was the popular prayer position then, rather than palms pressed together). The legend holds that the monk called his creation *bracellae*, Latin for "little arms." From there, Germans morphed the word into *bretzel*, which eventually evolved into "pretzel." Yet another story has it that the same legendary monk gave the tiny breads (which were soft-baked back then, like the stadium pretzels of today) to young children as reward for reciting prayers.

Andrea Slonecker, author of *Pretzel Making at Home*, says the pretzel is the symbol denoting a German bakery, displayed in wood or wrought iron. She likes the monk story to place the origin of the pretzel, but could not determine in her research which church deserves proper credit for this creation—so many stories now have spread through so many cultures. People tend to identify the pretzel as German-Lutheran in origin. But, other stories identify the origin as southern France or northern Italy during the seventh century. Experts from the Culinary Institute of America claim the soft pretzel has been in existence for 14 centuries. We do know that in the late 1800s, pretzels made their way to America from Germany and Austria. To this day, American pretzels are associated with Pennsylvania Dutch country, which was heavily settled by German immigrants. Millions are produced in factories every year, although hand-shaped pretzels are available in select bakeries and vendor carts from sporting events and fairs to city street corners. Pennsylvanians consume 12 times the amount of pretzels as the rest of America, Slonecker says. "Pretzels are very important to the Pennsylvania culture, especially Lancaster County."

Like the lore of the pretzel's origins, the shapes of pretzels now vary from sticks to circles and even waffle-shaped squares. But Slonecker says the original shape is clear: The dough was twisted into the shape of folded prayerful arms, creating three holes in the final bread. The shape has evolved into a religious representation of the Christian Trinity: Father, Son and the Holy Spirit. The Vatican Library has a manuscript illustrating one of the earliest pictures and descriptions of the pretzel.

Today, pretzels are mostly crispy, shiny and salty. Slonecker says the modern recipe includes dipping the pretzel into a food-grade lye solution (although many bakers use baking soda instead) to achieve the leathery chewiness. "You have to have an alkaline solution to get that effect," explains Slonecker. "Lye is much farther down the pH scale than baking soda so you can never get the same result with baking soda as you do with lye."

That was a case of mistaken brilliance, she notes. "A baker in Bavaria accidentally used the cleaning solution lye to glaze the pretzels before baking them, thinking it was this sort of syrupy concoction that they used to use," Slonecker says. "It was an accidental discovery—when it came out of the oven, they had this amazing dark color and chewy, leathery texture. I've read the science behind it—baking denatures the caustic substance in the food-grade lye."

"Pretzels will have more flavor and body if you let them rise uncovered in the refrigerator," said Chef Eric Kastel, Lecturing Instructor in Baking and Pastry Arts at The Culinary Institute of America (CIA), in an article on the subject provided with permission of the CIA. "When you allow the dough to rise slowly, the pretzel develops a thicker crust." Soft pretzels, along with many other desserts, are explained and illustrated in The Culinary Institute of America's *Baking and Pastry, Mastering the Art and Craft* cookbook, which was published in 2004.

Since soft pretzels are a church creation, where did hard pretzels come from? "An American baker who forgot them in the oven and they hardened," Slonecker says.

Slonecker's favorite way to eat pretzels? "Five minutes out of the oven, with salt."

Soft Pretzel Recipe

Makes 1 dozen large soft pretzels. If it is your first time making home-made pretzels, start with simple shapes because the more intricate the shape, the more difficult it is to dip in the solu-

tion prior to baking. Thinly rolled dough yields crispy pretzels and requires less baking time. Similarly, pretzels rolled thicker take longer to bake and are chewier. Experiment to determine whether you prefer crispy or chewy pretzels. Homemade soft pretzels are best eaten the same day.

For the dough:
2 envelopes (1½ tablespoons) active dry yeast
½ cup plus 1½ cups warm water
2 tablespoons brown sugar, packed
3½ tablespoons butter, softened
6 cups bread flour
1 tablespoon salt

For the dipping solution:
6 cups warm water
6 tablespoons baking soda
Coarse salt, for sprinkling

To make the dough: In the bowl of an electric mixer fitted with a dough hook, stir together the yeast, ½ cup of the warm water and a pinch of the brown sugar. Allow mixture to sit for 10 minutes. Add the remaining 1½ cups of warm water, brown sugar, butter, flour and salt to the yeast mixture. Begin mixing on low speed for 2 minutes and then on medium speed until the dough begins to pull away from the sides, about 2 to 4 minutes.

Turn out the dough onto a work surface and knead for about 5 minutes. The dough will be stiff, yet smooth. (**Note:** If mixing by hand, follow the same procedure for the yeast mixture. In a large mixing bowl, add the remaining ingredients in the same order listed above. Mix with wooden spoon until incorporated. Turn out onto work surface and knead for about 10 minutes. The dough will be stiff, yet smooth.)

Place dough into a lightly greased bowl and cover with a kitchen towel. Allow to double in volume, about 1 hour.

Punch down dough, transfer to work surface, and divide into 12 equal pieces. Form the dough into oblong pieces, cover with oiled plastic wrap, and let dough rest for 5 minutes. Line two cookie sheets with parchment paper and set aside.
Working with one piece at a time, roll dough by hand to 30 inches in length. (For traction when rolling, spray a fine mist of water on the work surface.) Lay the dough on the table in a U-shape and cross the ends over each other. Twist the ends together once. Bring the ends down and attach them to either side of the thicker center of the dough, pressing to seal them. For an on online video on twisting techniques, go to

Saveur.com (http://www.saveur.com/article/Video/Video-How-To-Twist-Pretzels)

Place pretzels on parchment-lined cookie sheets (6 per cookie sheet) and let rise, uncovered, for 25 to 30 minutes. Meanwhile, preheat oven to 450°F.

To make the dipping solution: Mix the baking soda and warm water in a stainless-steel bowl. Add a couple of pretzels at a time to the solution, allowing them to soak for 10 seconds. Lift out using a slotted spoon and place on the parchment-lined cookie sheets. Let pretzels dry slightly and sprinkle with coarse salt. Bake for 12 to 15 minutes, or until deep golden brown. Do not store in covered container.

Nutrition Analysis per pretzel: 290 calories, 9g protein, 52g carbohydrates, 4.5g fat, and 1080mg sodium.

—**Reprinted with permission from the Culinary Institute of America.**

chapter 3

Jewish Bread

Traditions of Joy, Gathering and Faith

IT'S THE HALLMARK of the weekly Sabbath, the inaugu-
ration of every holiday. It's a Jewish foundation in so many
ways. Challah. Its absence defines the Passover holiday.
More ritual is mandated before and after the consumption
of bread than any other part of daily life. Women around
the world bake bread weekly to celebrate the Sabbath and
many still follow a modified version of the biblical mandate
to "take challah," meaning charring a piece of dough beyond
recognition in memory of the High Priest in the Jewish
Temple. This is done because the Temple is no longer standing and thus the Jewish people are unable to perform the
sacrifices that took place there. Charring the dough recalls
the burning of a sacrifice. Plus, challah in Temple times was
central to the Temple service.

In the hierarchy of blessings a Jew recites before taking a
bite of food, the one for bread yields the largest after-story;
the *birkhat ha'mazon*, or grace after meals, is only recited in
full when the meal begins with a bite of bread.

I lived 10 years of my life as an Orthodox Jew and I learned the tricks of the trade. I always chuckled to see people opt out of including bread in a meal because they didn't have the time to do the full *bentshing*, as the *birkhat* is known colloquially. In such situations, inaugurating a meal with a bread that hadn't risen required only the *mazonot* prayer, a quicker intro with a much faster finale. There was the illusion of bread in a bite of a quick bread without the burden of the heavier prayers that came with a bread that had risen.

It's a funny world in which our blessings are dictated by what we eat—but I see the metaphor so clearly. A bread that rises takes time and care, attention to detail, ritual to create. It is heavier and settles more fully in the belly than a sweet bread or muffin made from the same ingredients but without the wait that yeast requires. These are the stories we tell ourselves around food, giving added significance to a weekend meal launched by bread, and I know I always savor that first bite as something special and extraordinary that I don't usually find during the week.

In Judaism, bread symbolizes joy, gathering and faith, abject trust in God, ultimate redemption and an absence of arrogance. The fluffy, yeast-risen challah that many Jews eat at every Friday dinner and every Saturday lunch to commemorate the weekly Sabbath is a generations-long tradition of bread baking—grandparents to grandchildren, parents to children—as a way of tangibly observing the rituals of a Jewish life.

Recipes abound. For Ashkenazim, or Jews whose ancestors hail from European or Russian origins, a typical Sabbath challah is sweet and braided, often topped with sesame seeds or poppy seeds. Sephardim, or Jews of Spanish or Oriental descent, bake flatbreads like pita to fulfill the *mitzvah* of challah.

Either way, the family, together for the Sabbath meal, lights candles then gathers around the table for *Kiddush*, the blessing over wine. In some homes, after the initial singing and blessings occur with wine, everyone leaves the table to ritually wash hands with a double-handled cup, usually purchased from a Judaica store or in Israel, to beautify the observance. A blessing is said over the hand washing and then everyone from youngest family member to the oldest remains silent until the first bite of sweet bread melts on the tongue.

In many communities, the person who blesses the challah sprinkles salt over the cut pieces to remind Jews that even in the best of times, there is sadness, due to the long-ago destruction of the Temple, which prevents Jews from continuing the Temple rituals and sacrifices.

On Rosh Hashanah, the Jewish new year, it is customary to bake challahs in round shapes—sometimes braided rounds, sometimes smooth—often filled with raisins and always dipped in honey to signify a sweet year. On holidays and on Sabbaths, Jews display two significant loaves, known as *lechem mishneh* that represent the double portion of manna God fed the Jews in the desert on Friday, so that nothing was made anew on the Sabbath. The challahs are covered with a cloth on the table, reminiscent of the manna, which was covered for protection by a layer of dew.

In modern times, we tell different stories to go with these rituals. Small children are taught that the challahs are covered because on every other day we bless the challah first before any other food. On the Sabbath, when *Kiddush* is recited first, parents tell their children that the challah loaves would be "embarrassed" to be shoved to second-best, so they are covered to avoid witnessing this turn of events.

Once each year, Jews make a big deal out of not eating bread. On Passover, which commemorates the Exodus from Egypt, Jews eat unleavened matzahs, crisp crackers made from flour and water mixed for no longer than 18 minutes to prevent any rising. So the story goes: The Jews left Egypt in such a hurry under Moses' lead, they did not have time to bake bread. It flattened and hardened into edible crackers, matzah, on the stones when they stopped briefly on their way to freedom.

Every year as Passover approaches, many Jews scour their houses to eliminate any crumbs or remnants of leavening. They clean and scour, switch dishes so they eat off plates and bowls that never held bread or other leavened foods. And for the duration of the weeklong Passover holiday, Jews stick to the strict interpretation, focusing their observance on these crunchy cakes.

According to teachings by the late Lubavitcher Rebbe (ruling head of a Hasidic dynasty), Menachem Mendel Schneerson, matzah is a "bread of poverty" symbolizing hardship when Jews were slaves in Egypt. (To read more about the symbolism of unleavened bread, see Chapter 6, page 61.) At the end of the Passover seder, the family eats the *afikoman*, or dessert portion of matzah. There are many customs and traditions around this. After the middle of three matzahs is broken at the beginning of the meal, one half is taken and designated as the *afikoman*. Most families wrap it in a cloth napkin to prevent breakage and then either the adults hide it for the children to discover later and barter to end the meal, or a well-meaning adult lets the kids "steal" it from his chair and hide it for adults to find.

Regardless, the meal cannot end without the "dessert" of the *afikoman*, so if it has been hidden, someone must locate it and negotiate to get it back. Some families give rewards to whomever succeeds in making a deal—gift certificates, books, silver dollars, toys for the little ones—but then every person at the table takes a tiny piece of this special matzah to close the *seder*. Some scholars say the *afikoman* represents the future redemption, which is yet hidden from the Jews. It is eaten last, they say, because first we must feel the hunger and taste the passion for truth before we can hunger for our final redemption.

Sometimes a love for ritual comes through food. In fact, the rituals exist to give us tangible paths inward toward a higher purpose. It is true with children and it remains true for many into adulthood as well. In Jewish synagogues, adults offer lollipops to children as an enactment of the scriptural insistence on making Torah-learning "sweet." So, too, a holiday or Sabbath table is dressed prettily in an effort to "beautify the commandment" (*hiddur mitzvah*) and laden with sweet, warm bread beckons to young and old alike, making the tradition sweet and memorable.

Maggie Glezer, author of some of the best-known bread-baking books in the Jewish community, came upon challah not from a place of religious mandate but first from a love of baking. "I always loved to bake," says Glezer, who may have loved the act of baking but wasn't quite successful with it. Desperately wanting to understand the technical aspect of making bread, Glezer spent a year poring over books at the University of Arizona's agricultural library (where her husband was a professor), until she "cracked this nut" enough to become expert in bread baking.

Bread baking truly is both art and science. "On the face of it, bread seems so easy and so basic—and in a way it is, but in a way it's unbelievably complex," says Glezer. "I had been at home with my son trying to be a stay-at-home mother and going crazy." This was more than 22 years ago, and Glezer had no intention of becoming the voice of Jewish breads. In fact, after her first book debuted, the family's rabbi asked if she was baking challah every week. Since she wasn't, she took it as an invitation to enter that genre and begin connecting the art of bread baking with the Jewish ritual aspects of making and sharing food.

Glezer is now a member of the Bread Bakers Guild of America. But, before she got into bread, she was in the dark about the Jewish laws, folklore and customs related to bread. Throughout the Diaspora, communities where Jews have scattered around the world, bread has morphed and evolved to combine ancient tradition with local flavors. Indeed, the large East-West divide means that, each week, entire Jewish communities bless pita-like flatbread while other equally Jewish communities bless the light, airy, sweet egg bread more universally associated with what is known as challah.

If you want to get down to brass tacks, the term "challah" in the Torah refers to the ritual of taking an olive-sized piece of dough and burning it in the oven until it is inedible. There is a blessing the person recites before doing so. This act recalls the Temple Service in Jerusalem, when the tribes baked breads for the *Kohanim*, or High Priests, something modern Jews can no longer do.

For her book, *A Blessing of Bread: Recipes and Rituals, Memories and Mitzvahs*, which features challah recipes, Glezer traveled from community to community in search of stories and breads to include. Now based in Atlanta, Glezer interviewed a local food writer who shared her wonderful stories, delicious recipes and inspiring traditions of how bread brought together people of varying, and even opposing, cultures: "I felt like I was an insurance salesman—inviting myself into people's homes and having them bake bread for me."

The stories she gathered opened Glezer's eyes to the complexities of the Jewish world in general. Her Israeli husband showed one face, that of Ashkenazi Holocaust survivors, but when Glezer began talking to North African Jews about their experiences, about how they were treated in Israel, she realized the politics of diversity. Challah in one Jewish kitchen looks very different from challah in another Jewish home, though it all stems from the same religious mandate and tradition.

When Glezer began her pursuit of challah from the perspective of the science of baking, she realized she had to learn about the observances and meanings behind this universal bread. "I had the typical Sunday School education," she says. "What shocked me was the fact that there is no absolute. I am still shocked that challah is also a *mitzvah*, an observance, and there is no agreement on the correct way to observe it. You have to follow a rabbi, and they do not agree and there is no way for them to ever agree because the measurements that the observance is based on are Talmudic and have been lost."

Glezer spent three years researching and learning before publishing *A Blessing of Bread*. Truth be told, says Glezer, there are hardly any truly unique Jewish breads. "They all have their roots in local customs; we do relate to our neighbors and learn from them, borrow from them, there is a back-and-forth. Even our braided challah is not something we invented; that's a German tradition."

In her book, Glezer recounts the story of a Moroccan custom called *Mimouna*, an open house to celebrate the end of Passover. A woman named Yaffa Peles told Glezer how their Muslim neighbors would bring the first flour after the holiday to their house, and Jew and Muslim alike would commune over tea and sweets. Bread was a bridge-builder, a peacekeeper, where flour was the symbol of our inherent "inter-relatedness," Glezer says. "There's a reason that the breads are the same."

Making challah as a family can be a symbolic way to live one's Judaism. Joe Lewis did this when his children were young. A Jewish author with his own small publishing house in Oak Park, Michigan, Lewis started baking bread when he and his wife, Bobbie, were in graduate school in Philadelphia. "My first attempt at making challah, and we still have a photo of it," he says, "was basically good for a doorstop."

When a baker's strike broke out in Philadelphia, Joe and Bobbie started making bread for sale to other graduate students. As the years went on, he experimented with recipes he found in books, newspapers and online, eventually creating his own amalgamation. He cites a "famous recipe for all families who went to Hillel Day School" in Farmington Hills, Michigan. "Mrs. Thatch's recipe. She was a teacher, and the kids always loved her, and since she was a Holocaust survivor, everything she said carried a lot of weight. Her recipe is great, but it uses a lot of oil," Lewis recalls.

Eventually, for his own baking, he settled on a recipe from Frieda Rita's *The Challah Book*. "She's got a method as well as a recipe. She says, 'Do things in this order and it'll work out well' and it does work out well."

Mrs. Riva Thatch's Challah Recipe

Makes 2 large or 4 small challahs. "Bread is the staff of life," says Aviva Sandler, Riva Thatch's daughter, who gave her blessing to include this long-loved rec-

ipe here. (Mrs. Thatch now suffers from Alzheimer's disease.) "Bread is what keeps people alive." Sandler first found a version of this recipe in a cookbook by Jenny Grossinger, wife of the owner of the well-loved Catskills resort, Grossinger's, where East Coast Jews flocked in summer to cavort and celebrate and gather for decades. "I made it three times, and my mother made it forever," says Sandler. "I'm sure she did a little tweaking. Every recipe becomes yours." Sandler and her parents are Holocaust survivors. Mrs. Thatch shared this recipe widely during her many years as a beloved teacher at Hillel Day School in Farmington Hills, Michigan.

8 cups bread flour
2 envelopes active dry yeast
⅓ cup sugar
1¾ cups warm water, divided by pouring out ⅓ cup of the total into a second measuring cup
4 eggs, plus 1 egg, lightly beaten
¾ cup oil
1 tablespoon salt

In a large bowl, add flour and make a well in the center. In a glass, mix the yeast with a little of the sugar plus ⅓ cup of the water and pour into the flour well. Sprinkle with a little of the flour. When it bubbles, add remaining ingredients and knead for about 8 minutes. Cover with plastic wrap, and let rise until doubled in size.

Punch down the dough. Cover with plastic wrap and let rise again until doubled in size. Line baking pans with parchment or brush with oil. Set aside.

Turn the dough onto a floured surface. If making 2 loaves, divide in two. Taking one piece, divide that into 3 equal pieces. Roll each piece into a log, and place the 3 logs parallel to one another. Weave the 3 strands into a tight braid, tugging as you go. Press the ends together to seal. For an online video on braiding techniques, go to Youtube (http://www.youtube.com/watch?v=YR6aIAh2Vt8). Place the loaf on prepared baking sheet. Follow the same procedure for second piece of dough. Cover both loaves with oiled plastic wrap and allow to rise until doubled in size. Meanwhile, preheat oven to 350°F.

Brush loaves with beaten egg gently but thoroughly, and bake until golden brown, about 20 to 30 minutes.

Holiday Hints from Riva: For Rosh Hashanah, I make them round and put a ladder on top so that our prayers could "climb up to heaven."

For Yom Kippur, I make a strip, fold it over and cut

fingers. This represents hands, our asking each other for forgiveness.

For Sukkot, I try to make fruits and vegetables. I also make flowers that can be used for Shavuot.

Maggie Glezer's Olive Oil Challah

Makes two 1-pound loaves or 1 half-pound loaf plus three 2-oz. rolls. Note: Prior to baking, the loaves/rolls must be refrigerated for 8 to 24 hours.

1 teaspoon instant yeast
3¾ cups bread flour
1¼ cups warm water
½ cup extra-virgin olive oil, plus more for plastic wrap
2 teaspoons table salt
Sesame seeds, for sprinkling

In a large bowl, whisk together the yeast and 1¼ cups of the flour, then whisk in the warm water until smooth. Let the slurry (semiliquid mixture) stand uncovered for 10 to 20 minutes, or until it begins to ferment and puff up slightly.

Whisk the oil and salt into the puffed yeast slurry until it is smooth and the salt has dissolved. With your hands or a wooden spoon, stir in the remaining 2½ cups flour all at once. When the mixture is a shaggy ball, scrape it out onto your work surface and knead until it is well mixed, fairly smooth and soft. (Soak your mixing bowl in hot water now to clean it and warm it for fermenting the dough.) If the dough is too firm, add a tablespoon or two of water to it; if it seems too wet, add a few tablespoons of flour.

The dough should be soft and glossy, and greenish if you used highly pigmented olive oil.

When the dough is fully kneaded, place it in the warmed clean bowl and cover it with oiled plastic wrap. Let the dough ferment until it has tripled in bulk, 2 to 3 hours, depending on the temperature in your kitchen.

Line a large baking sheet with parchment paper or foil; oil the foil. Divide the dough in half for two loaves or into one large piece for a large loaf plus three smaller pieces for rolls. Braid or shape them as desired, and position them on the prepared sheet. Cover well with oiled plastic wrap. Refrigerate the shaped loaves for at least 8 hours, or up to 24 hours.

About 2½ hours before you are ready to bake, remove the loaves from the refrigerator and let them proof until tripled in size.

Meanwhile, 30 minutes before baking, arrange an oven rack in the upper third position, remove any racks above it, and preheat the oven to 425°F. If you wish, you can preheat a baking sheet in the oven to double with the baking sheet the loaves will be on.

When the loaves have tripled and do not push back when gently pressed with your finger but remain indented, generously brush them with water, and then sprinkle them heavily with sesame seeds. Bake rolls for about 30 minutes, the smaller breads for about 40 minutes, or the larger loaf for about 50 minutes, until they are dark golden brown. Midway through the baking time, switch the breads from front to back so that they brown evenly. Transfer baking sheets to a rack to cool.

Option: Glezer's Olive Oil Challah Using Five Pounds of Flour

Makes 6 to 8 loaves.

2 envelopes (1 tablespoon plus 1½ teaspoons) instant yeast
5 pounds bread flour
5⅔ cups warm water
2⅓ cups extra-virgin olive oil
3 tablespoons table salt
Sesame seeds, for sprinkling

Mix dough and proceed as directed in previous Glezer recipe, but use 5⅔ cups of flour in the first step then add the rest of the bag of flour in the next step.

chapter 4

Native American Breads

Tenacity in Centuries of Shared Memories

PART SYMBOL OF oppression, part staple—Native American breads represent tradition, pained history and the inherent nurturing of a community. Frybread is a particular lightning rod. In 2005, Indian activists in South Dakota successfully lobbied to have it declared the official state bread. The food is a staple in Native American communities across the continent and is a popular treat at public gatherings like pow-wows. But, some activists are pushing back, arguing two main issues: Frybread is a fatty, high-carb food that contributes to chronic problems with obesity; and frybread is associated with colonization and oppression of native tribes by encroaching Europeans.

While he acknowledges truths in these arguments, Nephi Craig says bread remains an important cornerstone in Native American life. Part self-taught and part formally trained in culinary arts, Craig is executive chef of the restaurant at the Sunrise Park Resort, a large ski resort run by the White Mountain Apache tribe high in the Arizona mountains. "The pan-Native American one—frybread—is very familiar to all tribes and it has a lot of history. The common thread that I've observed going from tribe to tribe is there's a lot of humor associated with frybread: stories, jokes and sentimental value attached to a grandmother's recipe."

Native Americans are aware that it isn't healthy, he acknowledges. "And, historically, almost all of the ingredients in frybread are not indigenous to the Americas," Craig says. "So it is definitely a foreign food. A lot of it has to do with conquest and colonization and military rations and the introduction of the pig from the Spanish, where we first got lard."

Craig is leading a movement to canonize and promote Native American foods, frybread among them. He founded the Native American Culinary Association (NACA) in 2003 to publicize the creativity and flavor of the foods enjoyed by tribes in various regions of the country. The grassroots effort connects Native American chefs across America with momentum to create programs and collaborations that build awareness of authentic foods, some local and indigenous and others imported from interlopers, like the bread.

"When I first started cooking, I wasn't aware of any native chefs out there," he admits. "All I knew was all the non-native chefs who are very famous and I saw a huge gap and misrepresentation of us."

As Craig talks about native foods, he points to our universal taste for foods associated with home. As children, we take little notice of the legacies that provide the foods we enjoy. Yet, in every community, as one matures and ventures outside to experience new textures and flavors, that's when the context of what was once taken for granted is finally understood.

In the Native American world, bread can be part of ritual and observance—or simply a reminder of life's daily challenges. "A lot of breads are connected to humility," Craig says. "It's filler where there are not a lot of other foods or meats—just bread, and soup."

Ash bread is tied to the sunrise dance ceremony, celebrating funerals and births. Craig explains. It is "a very important ritual of sending someone home. As food to take with them on their journey through the universe or spirit world, one last piece of ash bread is made and placed on the grave or in the casket." It is a large amount of dough placed in the embers, sometimes mixing with the charcoal dust of the fire.

Ash bread dough itself is quite basic—flour, salt and baking powder. "I'm sure some people get technical and use yeast or milk, but that's the basic recipe," Craig says.

This important Apache rite has played a pivotal role throughout Craig's life. "When a baby laughs for the first time, we'll have a party, and normally whoever makes the baby laugh has to throw the party," he says. Ash bread is part of the menu. It appears when people gather, including at a coming-of-age ceremony for a young woman.

"Taking an honest, unbiased look at our foods enables me to look at both sides," says Craig. "It can be seen through a lens of oppression and colonization and conquest. That's very real and then you see the negative impacts of this food on public health—diabetes, obesity, poverty."

But, he argues: "Bread also represents tenacity, humility, adaptation of cultures and how important food is in general—not just to Native American culture, but to human beings and the family unit. It just changes the whole meal when someone brings in a big stack of bread, freshly made tortillas or frybread made by someone you love. It changes the whole energy of the dinner."

Bread also ties into the matriarchs of the Native American world, who "did what they had to do with what was available. These beautiful tasty things have become to me an embraced part of our culture," Craig says.

"Usually, the best things in the world are the most simple," says Craig. "And the most simple things have the most meaning attached to them, and bread is one of those things."

Simple? Yes. The same across the continent? No. In Washington, D.C., a highlight of any visit to the National Museum of the American Indian is a meal at the restaurant called Mitsitam Café (*mitsitam* means "let's eat!"). In one location, chefs offer a rotating menu of foods from different regions of the country and the tribes that live there.

In fact, at a recent visit to the Smithsonian's National Museum of the American Indian, my family learned more in the Mitsitam Café than in the exhibits. Indeed, we spent more than $100 on lunch alone as we tasted and tested a wide variety of colors, flavors and scents. It was such a journey that we emerged feeling as if we had truly experienced the Native American world simply by sampling its flavors. We are eminently familiar with the idea of food as significant, symbolic and full of meaning. And suddenly, in this knowing, our worlds were merged. The universality among us became clear.

Native American breads vary based on ingredients, climate and season, Craig explains. There are very thin tortillas cooked on a piece of metal; thick fluffy tortillas cooked in a flat, cast-iron skillet; frybread; and even a corn bread (not common, but a favorite sometimes sold door-to-door in the community). The corn bread is enriched with fresh corn scraped off the cob in summer or fall and mixed with flour, baking powder and salt, then lightly pan-fried until its hue darkens into a caramelized unleavened treat, sweetened only by the corn.

Craig is part White Mountain Apache (his mother's side), part Navajo (his father's side). He's lived in the White Mountain Apache tribe his entire life. "We are a matrilineal society," he explains. "I've been cooking my whole life, ever since I was a kid. I always enjoyed the act of making something tasty. And then I was reinforced by people cooking in my home or people cooking in my life."

Craig's grandfather, Joseph Ivans, grew a large garden down by a river in his community and he taught young Nephi how to cultivate and celebrate life through growing tomatoes, squash, plums and peaches. "I tended the garden regularly," he recalls. It made all the difference, since so many of his compatriots mainly ate foods rationed by the government, which were often packaged and processed.

"There is a profound difference between the commodities we had when we were real poor and the fresh food available now supplemented by the garden," he says.

The importance of home-prepared foods, especially bread, extends from one generation to the next. When his father died just a few years ago, Craig's mother made ash bread for him. "It was sad, it was really tough," he recalls quietly. "My father was a very well-known singer and songwriter in Indian country, Vincent Craig." He also wrote a comic strip called *Mutton Man*, which Craig insists was "more powerful than the BIA (Bureau of Indian Affairs and a longtime nemesis of Native American activists). Dad was influential. His passing was a huge loss to Indian country because he was an amazing character. We made ash bread to send with him through the universe."

Now, Craig is the influencer—leading others in the culinary traditions and trends of his community and preserving those traditions so they will never be lost. He is teaching the same powerful lessons to his son, to his kitchen staff and to anyone he encounters who will listen to a little story about the wonders and the magic of bread.

Tsigist'ii (Apache name for Beverly Malone's Tortillas)

Makes 10 to 14 tortillas. This bread is made year-round.

4 cups all-purpose flour
1 teaspoon baking
    powder
2 tablespoons salt
2 cups warm water

In a large bowl, mix together the flour, baking powder and salt. Gradually add the water. Mix until the dough comes together. Add more flour if dough is too tacky and sticks to your hands. Turn out onto lightly floured work surface. Knead the mixture several times. Divide into 10 to14 small balls. Let rest about 5 minutes.

Flatten the dough by stretching and patting by hand. Pieces should be about 5 inches in diameter. Shapes may be irregular.

Cook on top of a stove over high heat using a dry, cast iron pan or outdoors over hot coals of an open fire until lightly browned.

—**Printed with permission from the Nohwike' Bagowa Museum, Fort Apache, Arizona**

***

Here is a wonderful variation on cornbread with nuts and maple syrup from writer, chef and food stylist Annabel Cohen.

Maple Pecan-Topped Buttermilk Cornbread

Makes one 8x8 inch pan.

2 tablespoons canola or
    other vegetable oil, for
    pan
1 cup cornmeal
1 cup all-purpose flour
½ teaspoon salt
½ teaspoon baking soda
½ cup (1 stick) butter
¼ cup sugar
2 large eggs
1 cup buttermilk
1 cup pecan halves or chopped pecans
½ cup real maple syrup

Preheat oven to 375°F. Line the bottom of an 8x8-inch
baking dish with parchment. Spray the sides of the pan
and parchment with nonstick cooking spray; set aside.

Combine cornmeal, flour, salt and baking soda in a
bowl and whisk well; set aside.

Place butter in a large microwave-safe bowl. Cook
on high for 1 minute or until the butter is completely
melted. Stir in the sugar, eggs and buttermilk until uniform. Stir in the flour mixture until just incorporated
(do not over mix).

Transfer the batter into the prepared pan. Press the
pecans over the batter and drizzle with maple syrup.

Bake until the cornbread is golden and a toothpick inserted in the center comes out clean, about 30

minutes. Allow to cool for at least 10 minutes before cutting into squares and serving.

chapter 5

Breads Building a Mosque

How a Community Rose with Weekly Bread

ON A COOL fall Sunday, I arrived at the Islamic Center of America (ICA) in Dearborn, Michigan to watch the women bake bread. The minarets of the mosque soared to the sky, as if piercing the clouds above. I whisked inside, all smiles, eager to learn about a tradition different from my own. I was greeted with a welcoming smile and warm embrace by Fay Hamood, her head covered by a scarf and her face beaming. "Here," she beckoned. "Wear this."

I wrapped a black silken scarf around my curly hair so that only my face showed. Sheepish, this covering felt so familiar. After spending nearly a decade in the Orthodox Jewish community, I was acquainted with the ways in which women cover themselves out of religious respect. I looked at my reflection in the glass of a display case. I looked lovely, radiant, as if I held a secret inside my scarf. Funny, I'd never felt that way wearing my Orthodox hats. Perhaps it was the excitement and adventure of stepping into someone else's world that created that aura of mystery.

The floors gleamed as we walked past the lobby toward a banquet hall in the back of the building. I peeked into the round hall used for community prayers with its lush carpeting. On a wall, I noticed a golden tree with branches for sponsors' names—so similar to my faith's tree of life, also an exhibit of generous donors. I spotted words on a plaque beside the bathroom, speaking of *tahara*, purity. Interesting that the Hebrew for purity is *taharat*.

Before Fay and her sister Nancy Makki led the baking crew at the ICA, their mother, Hajjah Manifeh Dakroub, led the effort for half a century at what was known then as the Joy Road Mosque in Detroit. Every Friday night and every Sunday at 2 a.m., a dozen women from the community arrive at the mosque's commercial kitchen to mix flour and water and spices into the bread that parishioners flock to purchase. So simple, bread baking. And yet, this single repetitious act of solemn nourishment has kept the mosque afloat for more than 50 years.

Imam Hassan Qazwini, the mosque's spiritual leader, says the women of this mosque generate more than $200,000 every year from bread sales alone. "They are the backbone of the ICA," says the imam. "If it wasn't for them, maybe we couldn't have made it so far."

The ladies won't share their exact recipe, but the recipe at the end of this chapter is for a similar dough to the one they make twice weekly. A devoted secretary to the imam suggests that traditional Middle Eastern *baharat* spices, found at many specialty stores, might come close. The spice mixture is at once sweet, smoky, husky and comforting. Many have tried to guess the combination of ingredients, but the women at the mosque are very protective of their secret in order to keep this bread special and unique.

The mosque in Dearborn was built in 2005 to replace the Joy Road Mosque, which was created in the early 1960s. It is one of the largest mosques in North America, with a population of worshipers who are largely Lebanese (60-70%). The rest of the parishioners are a mixture of U.S.-born and immigrants.

Imam Qazwini was born in Iraq in 1970, but much of his family fled the country after his relatives were killed under the persecution of Saddam Hussein. He studied in Iran from 1980-1992, finishing with the Muslim religious equivalent of a PhD. He has led this community for 15 years. Active in interfaith work, Imam Qazwini has spoken to more than 300 congregations of nearly every faith, as well as colleges and universities, aiming to build bridges between Muslims and people of other faiths.

As we talk, Imam Qazwini thumbs through his smart phone, looking for Quranic references to food, hospitality and bread. He comes up with so many, offering them like tiny bites of sweetness.

"In the Quran, God mentions food numerous times," says Imam Qazwini. "Bread is mentioned only once—in a story about Joseph. When he is in prison, a man has a dream in which he is carrying bread and a bird is eating from the bread. He asks Joseph for an interpretation of the dream."

Overall, the sharing of food—which of course includes bread—is urged repeatedly in Muslim sacred writing from the Quran to the Hadith (the sayings of the Prophet Muhammad). In the Quran's chapter 106, often spelled *Quraysh* in English, God speaks to tribes who are standing defiantly against the Prophet Mohammad: "So let them serve the Lord of this house who feeds them against hunger and gives them security against fear."

"God is trying to say: Worship Him after He feeds us and secures us," says Imam Qazwini. "God is reminding us that He created us, He fed us, He sustained us, He took care of us, so then we have to worship Him. God offers bread, and He demands obedience."

In other Quranic verses, God asks Muslims to feed the poor and take care of the needy, the imam says. "The Prophet Mohammad tells a moving story. Ibrahim had guests over. He had the tradition to have his house open for strangers. He offered food to a stranger and as the stranger was about to eat, Ibrahim said, 'Let's say a prayer.' The guest says, 'Pray to who?' The guest didn't know God; he was an atheist. Ibrahim was very offended, so he said, 'Forgive me, I cannot allow you to eat my food.' And the man left.

"After that, God sent the angel Gabriel to Ibrahim, admonishing him. God said, 'I fed him 50 years and I didn't ask him to recognize me. I feed even my enemy.'

"Ibrahim apologized. He went and found the man and said, 'The God you don't believe in is admonishing me for not feeding you.'"

The lesson Imam Qazwini draws from this? Muslims believe that God's generosity must be extended to the world by believers who will help to feed others in need.

People certainly are fed at the Islamic Center. Each week, community members place their orders for bread, some buying more than they need so they can ship these tasty loaves all over the country. The recipe for this bread, *ba'at,*

follows a cultural tradition with no expressly religious con-
notation. The women also make cookies known as *ka'ak
al'Eid*, sweet, savory, chewy disks made from butter, sugar
and milk. The molds that make the delicate surface designs
came from Lebanon.

Almost as soon as you enter the mosque, you can smell
the sweet enveloping scent of the bread baking. Although
the mosque offers a Sunday breakfast, with a talk by the
imam, "what gets them here is the bread," says Fay. "They sit

down to listen and buy bread."

This bread is served at breakfast with cheese, boiled eggs and olives, or as a late night snack with tea, she says. It's served any time a group gathers in the mosque and also one night during the fasting month of Ramadan—a special evening often called the Great Night of Power. Usually marked during the second half of the month-long fast, the Great Night of Power recalls a time when the angel Gabriel brought the Holy Quran down to the Prophet Mohammad. As the story goes, the sky opens up and Muslims pray all night to wish for good outcomes, Fay explains. Then while it is still dark, they eat the bread, hot out of the oven, before starting another all-day fast.

"On that night, we serve 1,000 people," she says. "And the bread is always fresh."

Ramadan is perhaps the best-known Muslim observance. The month of fasting, according to Muslim scholars, is intended to focus the mind on others, explains Imam Qazwini. "When we are full, we cannot understand hunger. God says, 'When I make you hungry, now you know the pain.' Then we are motivated to give. We starve ourselves voluntarily so we are more motivated to give, to feed the poor."

In Islam, feeding others is "one of the most noble deeds" in God's eyes, the imam notes. In every religion, truly, these values are shared. They are one of the universal truths that create bridges between all communities of faith.

Muslims say no special prayers before taking a bite of bread, says Imam Qazwini, but they do recite a very brief grace over a main meal. And meals nearly always include bread.

How did the bread baking become such a mainstay in the mosque's annual budget? Christians and Jews are familiar with weekly pledges or annual giving among members of a congregation. But Islam does not have a tradition of membership associated with individual mosques. There are no dues. People do not tithe. Major donors do make gifts. Many people contribute smaller amounts throughout the year. The ICA does reach out to a mailing list of 3,000 households, representing at least 15,000 people, for two fundraisers to support the mosque each year. But, season after season and year after year, the bread-baking revenue has closed gaps in the budget, kept the doors open and contributed to new construction.

Islamic Center bread baking began when Hajjah Manifeh Dakroub initiated a fundraiser at the Joy Road Mosque more than 50 years ago. "The thing that brought people together most was bread and cookies," says Fay. "The proceeds from bread sales were significant."

Members from the mosque's women's club gather in the middle of the night to begin the process. By 6:30 a.m., more women arrive, jumping in to help and starting on the cookie dough, too. On Sundays, the women make five 50-pound loads of bread and on Fridays they bake four 50-pound loads. They make cookies on Sunday only, usually three 50-pound loads. (Each load makes 75 bags of finished cookies or bread.)

Their food processor dough recipe, included at the end of this chapter, is a good base for their popular bread. "The secret in all of this is the spices," says Fay. The women make their own mix of spices and won't disclose what it includes. Cardamom? Nutmeg? Who knows? "People are trying to figure it out."

Three days before Fay and Nancy's mother died, they went to sit with her in the hospital. "She sat up in the bed and asked, 'Did you order flour?'" Fay recalls. "I said, 'No, but I will.' She said, 'You have to!' She could hardly speak. I said, 'Ma, you don't have to worry.' And she reached over and handed me the telephone. I assisted her in dialing. She then grabbed the phone out of my hand and ordered flour."

After their mother's passing, Fay and Nancy had to piece together the recipe their mother had been producing at the mosque for so many decades. "My mother had five sisters," says Fay. "She gave each a bit of the recipe. We pulled it together."

Hajjah Manifeh Dakroub came to the United States from Lebanon in 1948, through Ellis Island. She gave birth to Fay on the boat coming over. One of Fay's brothers served as a U.S. soldier in the Korean War; in all, there are seven children. Their mother was a fixture in the mosque kitchen for every fundraiser, every gathering. "Everyone loved her food," says Fay. "It was the best of the best."

Hajjah Manifeh was a co-founder of the Women's Auxiliary of the Islamic Center. "Dad was Mom's right hand—he would get ingredients for her and never complain, because it was for the mosque," she recalls.

Fay has retired from a career at Ford Motor Co. Her sister Nancy is retired from a career in the Dearborn Public Schools. Their father worked for General Motors. A tiny gallery in a quiet corner of the mosque features display cases with photos and relics, representing the history of this mosque. An old photograph of Fay's parents is protected behind glass.

The women who come to help bake the bread are a microcosm of American assimilation. There are recent émigrés as well as American-born doctors, lawyers and judges. They come weekly, as dedicated as the women who set the path before them. Community members pay $3 per bag of bread, $6 for a dozen cookies. The ICA will freeze and ship orders anywhere in the country.

The mosque is quiet on a Sunday morning, though teeming with energy. The reassuring scent of nourishment hovers in the air. Every woman I meet wants to feed me. Some of the older women, huddled in headscarves and bent by age, their beautiful faces lined with wisdom, offer me home-cooked hard-boiled eggs, carted to the mosque in store-bought Styrofoam. "We take care of our guests," they tell me.

I choose a bag of the plain bread to take home to my family and a bag of bread coated with *za'atar*, my favorite Middle Eastern spice. The bread freezes well; it has a long shelf life, they tell me.

On her deathbed, Hajjah Manifeh made her daughters promise they would continue this tradition she started so long ago. "We make this in memory of our mother," says Fay. Now, Nancy has five children and 13 grandchildren; Fay has two children and two grandchildren. The tradition will continue with the new generations, they say, handed down as their mother envisioned.

Fay Hamood's Food Processor Bread Dough

Makes about 12 disks.
These round flat breads
are filling and delicious.
The spices make all the
difference, according
to Fay Hamood. A sug-
gestion is a fragrant
cinnamon-blend spice
with a hint of pepper
called "*baharat* 7spice,"
which can be found at
Mediterranean/Middle
Eastern markets. This
dough can also be used
to make traditional Mid-
dle Eastern meat pies.
The filling combines
cooked ground meat and a unique mixture of spices.

1 envelope active dry yeast
2 tablespoons sugar
1½ cups warm water, divided
4 cups flour (you can use a combination of all-purpose and
    bread flour)
½ cup corn or other vegetable oil, plus more for bowl
1 tablespoon spices
1 teaspoon salt

In a food processor, combine the yeast and sugar with
¼ cup lukewarm water. Pulse 3 times and let rest for 5
minutes until yeast becomes frothy.

Add remaining 1¼ cups warm water and the rest of the ingredients, pulsing until mixture balls up. Transfer the dough to a lightly oiled bowl and cover with plastic wrap. Let rise for 30 to 45 minutes.

On a lightly floured work surface, gently roll dough into 2-inch balls. Cover with plastic wrap and let set for another 45 minutes. Meanwhile, preheat oven to 350°F.

Using a floured rolling pin, shape each ball into a large, flat disk.

Bake on oiled or parchment-lined baking sheets for about 20 to 25 minutes or until lightly golden.

chapter 6

Sacred Breads

A Catholic Look at 2,000 Years of Spiritual Baking

FOR THE WORLD'S 2.2 billion Christians, bread recalls the founder of the faith: Jesus, who Christians believe instructed his followers to regularly eat a ritual meal of communion with God and other Christians. The Gospels report Jesus' actions and words involving bread and wine 2,000 years ago, so this might seem like a clear and universal practice—but communion rituals actually separate the Christian world. They divide Christians in belief, ritual practices and even the substance of the food to be consumed. For example, most Christians around the world sip wine in communion; but a sizeable minority of Christians use unfermented grape juice; and some even use water. Many Christian congregations celebrate communion at least once a week; other churches celebrate the ritual once a month or less. Most Christian churches strictly limit who is allowed to consume the communion elements; other congregations open the table to anyone who cares to partake. More than a matter of practice, communion traditions also deeply divide Christians in their core convictions about the meaning of bread and wine. Catholics believe that bread and wine consecrated in the Eucharist become the real body and blood of Christ—not visible as flesh and blood, but spiritually very real as body and blood of Christ as God. However, many Christians who split with Rome in the Reformation 500 years ago believe that the bread represents something else in communion—more of a symbol remembering Jesus. Huge theological tomes have been written about the differing doctrines on communion and, the chasms in belief are deep and emotionally held to this day. Within the United States, about 1 in 4 Americans is Catholic; 2 in 4 are Protestant. Visit various local churches on a series of Sunday mornings, and you will find a wide range of beliefs and practices.

Of course, what happens in the Roman Catholic Church shapes the whole world. After 2,000 years, the billion-plus men and women who adhere to the Catholic Church headquartered at the Vatican comprise the world's largest organized religious group. Circle the globe and attend Catholic Mass in any country you visit—and the Church's teaching about Eucharist is uniform.

"It all goes back to Jesus' commands at the Last Supper to 'do this in memory of me,'" says Father Dan Merz, associate director of the United States Conference of Catholic Bishops Secretariat of Divine Worship in Washington, D.C. Today, there are many recipes for communion wafers but in essence, they are all simple. Communion bread must be made of wheat flour and water, period. Roman Catholic custom dictates a thin round wafer, but there are no exact dimensions. The range is from 3 inches across to perhaps double that for the host used by the priest, so that all congregants can see it held aloft during the celebration of Mass.

The Vatican also has ruled that for the Eucharist to be valid, it must contain a miniscule percentage of gluten,

Father Merz explains. Gluten-intolerant Catholics do have options, though. The Benedictine Sisters in Clyde, Missouri, developed a low-gluten host that has such miniscule gluten content that parishioners with celiac disease or gluten intolerance may still take communion. Or, Catholics with these health challenges can receive communion in the form of consecrated wine alone, which the church teaches is "the whole Christ. The reason for communion of both kinds is simply a fuller symbol but if you just receive one, you receive the whole reality," clarifies Father Merz.

The debate over leaven in the host raged for centuries among ancient Christians. Western-rite Roman Catholic churches require unleavened bread; Eastern Orthodox churches use leavened bread. "For Catholic Christians, there is some evidence in the first several hundred years that we used leavened bread for the Eucharist but at some point in that first millennium, maybe in the 7th or 8th century, the Western church, the Latin-rite church, switched to unleavened bread," says Father Merz.

Christian Lessons in Unleavened Bread

"Unleavened bread was used in the Old Testament in the Jewish Temple. It was used by Jesus at the Last Supper. St. Paul himself, in 1 Corinthians, talks about 'Jesus is the new Passover, is the paschal lamb.' Christians, just like the Jews, were asked at the time of Passover by St. Paul to throw out the old leaven. He equates that old leaven was wickedness and evil; he says Christians should become 'fresh dough, unleavened,' for Christ." (To read more about the symbolism of matzah, see Chapter 3, page 27.)

Leaven was considered an agent of decay or deterioration, Father Merz notes. Ancient sources considered leaven as the "arch-symbol of fermentation, deterioration and death, thus taboo on the altar of blessing and life, the very place of God's presence." Unleavened bread symbolizes "starting over—making a break from a potentially sinful past and getting rid of the corruption of sin from our lives and our houses," he says.

"The Romans saw that. As well as in the Jewish Exodus, they were told to pack their bread before it rose, before it was leavened, and part of the reason for that was they were supposed to be ready to flee at a moment's notice.

"In several places in the Old Testament, God says: 'You don't have to do anything; just sit back and let me save you.' So unleavened bread includes that symbolism of inactivity, so that God can come and act on us, His power can be manifest," explains Father Merz.

The New Revised Standard Version—an English translation of the Bible read in many American churches today—renders the words of 1 Corinthians 5:7-8 as: "Clean out the old yeast so that you may be a new batch, as you really are unleavened. For our paschal lamb, Christ, has been sacrificed. Therefore, let us celebrate the festival, not with the old yeast, the yeast of malice and evil, but with the unleavened bread of sincerity and truth."

Christian Lessons in Leavened Bread

Eastern churches—and most Protestant churches—use leavened bread in communion. It's not a matter of right or wrong, Merz says, just custom and interpretation. Just as there are many places in Scripture relating leaven to decay, there are as many where Jesus uses leaven in a positive way. "In the Gospels, Jesus likens the kingdom of heaven to leaven, which will raise the whole world.

"The idea is that leaven is this agent of resurrection, a symbol of the Holy Spirit," explains Father Merz.

The New Revised Standard Version has two nearly identical passages—Matthew 13:33 and Luke 13:20-21—in which Jesus talks about leavening. The Matthew verse reads: "He told them another parable: The kingdom of heaven is like yeast that a woman took and mixed in with three measures of flour until all of it was leavened."

Such communion-related issues were part of the split between the Eastern and Western Christian Church in 1054. But, "today it's not a key issue. Today they say it's two different approaches of theology toward the same goal: Either focusing on the negative to get rid of sin and make ourselves pure and being ready for God's action with our inaction—or focusing more positively with leavened bread in terms of the power of the Holy Spirit and the power of the resurrection, the risen Christ."

To Salt, or Not to Salt?

Another long-running argument in the debate over communion bread centers around salt. Aristotle used salt as a metaphor for growing in friendship. A "covenant of salt" was understood in ancient times to refer to a permanent covenant. In 2 Corinthians 13:5, St. Paul refers to such a sign: "The Lord God of Israel gave the kingship over Israel for ever to David and his sons by a covenant of salt."

In general, Western churches do not include salt, but Eastern churches often do, Father Merz says. "Salt has often been an important ingredient in communion bread. Salt was such an important ingredient in the ancient world. It was a preservative. Jesus mentions it in several places: 'You are the salt of the earth … ' In the Acts of the Apostles, after the resurrection it says Jesus stayed with the Apostles for 40 days and instructed them. The literal Greek reading of the words is that 'He shared salt with them,' though it is translated as 'He met with them.'"

There is a sense of preservation in that language, Father Merz says. "He was sharing the Holy Spirit with them, preserving them in the truth, giving them the flavor of life, so to speak."

Other Altar Breads

Many Eastern churches have a custom of displaying not only the bread used for communion but also another bread that receives a priestly blessing. While the main communion liturgy is limited to church members—at the end of the liturgy, anyone can receive the other blessed bread, Father Merz says. This is not a part of the Latin-rite Catholic tradition, but Eastern-rite Catholic churches (churches with ancient roots in the Orthodox world that now are in union with the Vatican) do practice this community-building bread breaking.

St. Joseph's Bread, another kind of sacred bread, also is presented on special altar displays in Italian, Spanish, Maltese and some Filipino communities. The Blessing of St. Joseph's Table—often called St. Joseph's Altar—takes place during the Feast of St. Joseph on March 19. These temporary altars often are elaborately decorated with breads, statues, rosaries and flowers. The breads are lovingly made from long-standing family recipes and placed on the altars with special blessings.

At the end of that day, the breads are given to the poor. The custom dates to medieval times and the breads featured are mostly sweet breads. Jon Petrie, a New Orleans culinary expert, says the Sicilian tradition for St. Joseph's Bread goes according to this story: "Sicily was going through a terrible famine. The population made a pledge to St. Joseph that if he would deliver them from the famine, and they would erect a bountiful altar in his memory. That began the tradition. Since New Orleans was a port of entry for a lot of immigrants, and at one point a lot of Italian immigrants, particularly Sicilians, the west bank of the city became known as Little Italy. The tradition of St. Joseph's Altar came with those immigrants."

Today, individuals make pledges to St. Joseph for deliverance from difficult situations. They'll do it in their homes or as a community, in churches or community centers, Petrie says.

The breads vary in shape, size and flavor, but every item

on the altar has a strong religious significance. There are fig cakes, which are similar to Linzer tortes, with eyes cut out of the dough as a pledge to St. Lucia, the patron saint of eyes. There's pine cone- shaped fried dough dipped in hot caramel syrup, signifying "the pine cone Christ played with when he was a child." There's Milanese-style pasta sauce topped with breadcrumbs, the breadcrumbs symbolizing sawdust from Joseph's saw.

"It's considered good luck to get a piece of bread," says Petrie, and keeping it is a good luck charm, even if it becomes stale. "One of the more interesting superstitions is to get a piece of bread and when weather gets bad, throw it outside and the bad weather is supposed to go away."

Bread is everywhere in the Bible. Bread is a sustaining backbone of Christian tradition around the world. As a central symbol of faith, bread completes a timeless circle of separation and reunion. In the beginnings of Genesis, "it was by eating that our salvation was lost with Adam and Eve," says Father Merz. "In the same way, it is by eating that our salvation is recovered today with the celebration of the Eucharist."

St. Joseph's Bread

Makes one 2 pound, 12 ounce loaf. Malt syrup is a specialty product that can be found in health food stores.

2 envelopes (½ ounce)
   active dry yeast
2 cups water
¼ teaspoon malt syrup or
   honey
4½ cups bread flour
1 tablespoon salt
Sesame seeds, natural if
   possible, for topping

In the bowl of an electric mixer fitted with the dough hook, soften the yeast in the water. Let the mixture sit 1 to 2 minutes before proceeding.

Add the malt syrup (or honey), flour and salt, in that order to the softened yeast mixture. Beat on medium speed until dough is smooth. The dough should come away from the sides of the bowl and should have well-developed gluten or feel slightly tacky to the touch.

Turn out the dough onto a lightly floured work surface and finish kneading it by hand so that it forms a solid ball. Place in a lightly oiled bowl, cover with plastic wrap and set aside in a warm place to allow the dough to double. This may take as long as 1 hour.

Turn out the dough onto a lightly floured surface and divide it into 3 equal portions. Handling the dough gently at this point will make the next steps easier.

Working with one piece of dough at a time, roll it into a cylinder about 30 inches in length—the diameter is not as important as the length. Repeat the process with the remaining 2 pieces of dough.

Braid the strands of dough using a standard 3-braid procedure. For an online video on braiding techniques, go to Youtube (http://www.youtube.com/watch?v=YR6aIAh2Vt8.)

Lightly wet the top of the braided bread with water and sprinkle with or roll the top of the bread in the sesame seeds. There should be plenty of sesame seeds sticking to the bread at this point.

Place braided dough onto a parchment-lined baking sheet, lightly cover with plastic wrap and allow to proof (ferment) until the bread becomes puffy, about 30 to 45 minutes. (Be careful not to over-proof the dough at this stage or the baked bread will lack structure. To determine proper proofing, test by poking the dough. If it springs back immediately, it needs more time.) Meanwhile, preheat the oven to 425°F.

If desired, lightly mist the surface of the bread with water to produce a crisper crust; this is good if you are not baking with steam.

Bake until the crust is brown, 20 to 30 minutes. The bread should reach an internal temperature of 200°F on an instant-read thermometer, and should have a hollow sound when thumped on the bottom.

Hot Cross Buns

Makes 1 dozen buns. Around the English-speaking world, hot cross buns are one of the most popular seasonal sacred breads. Today's hot cross buns may have roots in pre-Christian Europe. Some historians say that pagans once made buns marked with a cross

to honor the goddess Eostre, and the cross symbolized the moon's four quarters. Springtime associations with Eostre were folded into the Christian Easter. In any case, hot cross buns have been associated with the Christian calendar for many centuries. Because the top of each bun is decorated with a cross, they are baked and enjoyed on Good Friday when Christians reflect on Jesus' crucifixion. The rich flavor made them popular with common people, who rarely enjoyed such treats throughout the year. The English nursery rhyme "Hot Cross Buns" celebrates street vendors who sold them hot from the oven: *If you have no daughters; Give them to your sons!*

For the dough:
**4 cups bread flour (you can use a combination of
    all-purpose and bread flour)**
1 teaspoon salt
3 teaspoons pumpkin pie spice
1 cup sugar

⅔ cup dark raisins
½ cup golden raisins
½ cup dried currants
1 envelope (2½ teaspoons) instant yeast
4 tablespoons butter
1 cup milk
1 egg, beaten

For the paste:
⅓ cup flour
4 tablespoons water
For the glaze:
½ cup sugar
3 tablespoons milk
3 tablespoons water

To make the dough: Sift together flour, salt and spices. Stir in sugar and dried fruits (You may use your hands for this to make sure all the dried fruits are broken up.) Stir in yeast; set aside.

Melt butter over low heat, stir in milk and heat until warmed through but not hot to the touch.

Add butter mixture to flour mixture and stir until dough is sticky and wet.

Turn the dough out onto a generously floured work surface. Knead it, adding enough flour to make it moderately stiff. Divide into 12 equal pieces. Shape dough into smooth balls. Place on oiled or parchment-lined baking sheet. Cover with a damp cloth or oiled plastic wrap. Let rest in a warm place until doubled in size. Meanwhile, preheat oven to 350°F.

For the paste: Mix together flour and water until it thickens. Using a pastry bag fitted with a plain round tip or a plastic bag with a corner snipped off, pipe one line of flour paste across the center of each bun, then a second line at right angles to the first, creating a "cross."

Bake about 20 minutes until golden brown. Do not overbake.

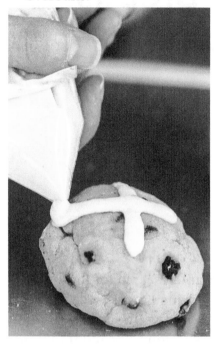

For the glaze: Heat sugar, milk and water gently in saucepan, stirring until sugar is dissolved, 2 or 3 minutes. Transfer buns to wire rack and immediately brush twice with glaze. Allow to cool completely.

—This recipe was adapted from one picked up by author Jane Wells in a British grocery store, Waitrose. Jane wrote *Glitter in the Sun: A Bible Study Searching for Truth in the Twilight Saga*.

chapter 7

The King of Breads

Discovering Baby Jesus in a Loaf of Bread

AS I COLLECTED interviews and research for this book, I became tempted to taste the varying flavors I was learning about. I could make the recipes myself—or I could find a way to immerse myself in the communities and traditions that gave birth to the recipes I was handed. As I researched the traditions of King Cake in New Orleans, I sent a quick email to my husband's cousin, Alex, who lives there, asking what he knew. A few days later, UPS knocked at the door with a rectangular box marked "perishable." Alex shipped a bona fide King Cake from the land of Mardi Gras to my doorstep far north. I pinged a quick note to his inbox: "I guess we're eating cake tonight."

The sweet coffeecake ring was glazed with colored sugar crystals in the hues of Mardi Gras: purple, gold and green. We cut generous portions, eating quickly with the hope that one of us would find the tiny plastic Baby Jesus figurine in our piece. No such luck. It wasn't until two days later, the cake mostly gone with just a piece or two left, that the baby simply fell out of the decimated cake, unceremoniously onto the kitchen counter. We laughed and looked at the tiny symbol before us: a naked baby made of plastic and meant to symbolize so much. Washed and dried, he perched on the windowsill above the kitchen sink until at some point he simply disappeared.

From the sublime mysteries of sacramental breads to the surprising delight of discovering a tiny Jesus in a handful of warm, sweet bread—that's the wondrous range of sacred baking traditions that now encircle our globe. From centuries-old theology fit for learned scholars to debate in seminaries to the simple pleasure of a child's laughter at the discovery of a plastic figurine at a family dinner table— that's the range of settings where bread points us toward spirit and connection.

So, we close our adventure in baking and in sharing sacred stories with this joyful practice that draws fond attention from aficionados like Jon Petrie in New Orleans.

When asked how many ceramic and plastic babies Jon Petrie has in his collection of King Cake prizes, he sighs and says simply, "a lot."

"When I first started collecting what I remembered of the King Cake baby, I would go to antique stores and buy them all up," says Petrie, assistant professor of culinary and pastry arts at Delgado Community College in New Orleans. A native New Orleanian, Petrie has collected all the pieces issued by the famous King Cake bakery, Haydel's, in addition to other gems he stumbles upon. "I'm building my own little Mardi Gras parade scene with them. There are marching bands and parade floats. Some friends have given me other miniatures in the same style of this but they would never have been included in King Cake as such."

Today, King Cake is mostly associated with the festival of Mardi Gras in New Orleans, but cultures around the world have developed cakes and breads with an auspicious surprise inside, some stemming from the ancient world.

These symbolic loaves may be associated—depending on the ethnicity and religious history of the community—with the arrival of Three Kings or Magi after the birth of Jesus, or with the start of the Lenten season that leads to Easter, or even with discovering Jesus hidden in a loaf—like Jesus emerging from the tomb on Easter. These days, it's possible to eat this kind of bread or cake and declare it a lesson on almost any part of the Christian calendar. Home cooks and eager consumers can be creative.

Beyond the Christian realm, the beloved tradition of Chinese mooncakes stretches back thousands of years. The idea involves carefully baking a whole egg yolk—and sometimes a special message—inside a beautifully decorated sweet or savory loaf. The golden yolk represents either the moon spirit or other spiritual themes. These cakes have become such an art form that few home cooks attempt to produce them. Today, a small box of traditionally prepared mooncakes fetches a price comparable to buying fine chocolates.

"In ancient times, tribes that survived the harshness of winter celebrated by baking a crown-shaped cake," Arthur Hardy, a New Orleans writer and top authority on Mardi Gras writes in *Mardi Gras in New Orleans: an Illustrated History.* The cake contained a seed, bean or nut. The Catholic Church appropriated this custom in the 4th century, Hardy says, and included it in the Feast of the Epiphany or Three Kings. By the 17th and 18th centuries, the *roi de la fève* (king of the bean) was celebrated in Europe, with "Twelfth cakes" baked in England.

The baking of Twelfth (Night) cakes, also known as *galette des rois* in French, is a Christian custom mostly observed in France, Belgium, Switzerland and England, says Chef Alain Levy, associate professor at the Culinary Institute of America (CIA) in Hyde Park, N.Y., and a native of Strasbourg, France. In observance of Epiphany, European bakers place a small porcelain baby figure, symbolizing the infant Jesus, inside the cake to represent the child honored by the Three Kings. The circular form of the cake symbolized the circuitous route of the kings to visit the holy baby.

The New Orleans custom of including a baby figure has become a free-for-all, with all sorts of figurines and even props and scenes included in some King Cakes. An authentic New Orleans King Cake, says Petrie, is made from cinnamon-roll dough.

The shape, name and taste of the cake vary from place to place. In southern France, this cake is called *fougasse,* a type of pastry topped with almonds and nuts; in eastern France it is comprised of three types of sponge cake, called *gateau de Savoie.* And in Lyons, brioche or yeast-risen dough is the base of the recipe. In some places it is a pound cake, while in Paris, the *galette feuilletée* is a round of puff pastry dough filled with almond cream. The Parisian custom is that whoever finds the bean inside has to buy wine and champagne for his friends.

The Land of King Cakes

Nowhere is King Cake as big a deal as in New Orleans. The ring-shaped sweetbread, decorated in the three official Mardi Gras colors, symbolizes a variety of things beyond the simple air of festivity that envelopes Mardi Gras.

The standard Mardi Gras colors reportedly symbolize justice, faith and charity or love, says Petrie. But really, they don't symbolize anything, he laughs, admitting that, actually, that's the meaning people have projected upon these colors that have so long been associated with the holiday.

Today, more than 500,000 King Cakes are consumed in New Orleans every year, with another 75,000 shipped out of state via overnight delivery. King Cake season begins on the twelfth day of Christmas, or January 6th, until Fat Tuesday, the day before Ash Wednesday. It's likely that the New Orleans King Cake tradition was inspired by French Twelfth Night cakes of old, compatible with New Orleans' French lineage, Petrie notes. Many New Orleans practices meld French customs with New World practice.

"In the everyday life of a typical New Orleanian, King Cakes will appear usually before Twelfth Night, after Christmas," Petrie says. "People refer to it as 'Little Christmas'. As tradition goes, someone buys the first one, and secreted inside the cake is a little plastic doll and whoever gets the baby is on target to buy the next King Cake, so throughout carnival season, if you get the baby, you buy the next one, and it propagates out the tradition of *let's have a party*, anything to celebrate food and eat."

There are others who believe that finding the baby simply forecasts good luck for the year to come. The New Year's tradition of finding an auspicious surprise in a special loaf is a longstanding custom in many parts of the world, especially in cultures that associate their New Year with the start of the spring season.

In New Orleans, the discovery of the prize helps to select the queen of Rex, one of the most prestigious Mardi Gras roles, Petrie says. The folks who run the Rex organization hide a gold bean into one of the pieces of cake and silver beans in a bunch of others and whoever finds them is chosen for the parade court. The tradition continues, but the outcome actually "is all pre-selected," Petrie says. Rex organizers know who will be chosen as queen among girls in society circles. The anointed girl is sure to receive the piece of cake carrying a gold bean. Silver bean recipients become maids of her Mardi Gras court.

King Cake babies have become a curious art form. The traditional piece was that of a Christ Child wrapped in swaddling clothes—and any white icing used atop the cake similarly symbolized this purity of the Christ Child's arrival.

Ceramic babies during World War II gave way to plastic babies by the 1960s, largely because people were biting down on the ceramic and breaking teeth, Petrie says. The first New Orleans King Cake baby was a frozen Charlotte doll; legend has it that the tiny china doll was inspired by a pious little girl who froze to death seeking the Christ Child, says Hardy.

"Some bakeries insert it before baking and some insert it

after baking," says Petrie. "I'd advise people to put the baby in afterwards because there's a big debate about baking with a piece of plastic in a cake." (Beware that if you add a tiny plastic item to the cake after it finishes baking, everyone will know where it is: inserting it before baking guarantees the cake will rise around it and it will be more of a surprise to discover.)

Twelfth Night Cake (*Galette des Rois*)

Makes one 11-inch cake. While there are several versions of this cake available, this particular one is most similar to the Parisian-style *galette feuilletée* using puff pastry and filled with a delicious almond cream. **Note:** For ease in flipping the cake, cut 2 discs, one 11 inches and one 12 inches, out of cardboard or foam core.

1 package frozen, store-bought puff pastry dough
2 cans (8 ounces each) almond paste
2 sticks (1 cup) unsalted butter
¼ cup granulated sugar
4 eggs, plus 1 for wash
3 tablespoons flour, plus more for dusting
1 tablespoon plus ½ teaspoon vanilla or rum extract (use up to 3 tablespoons, if desired)
1 plastic/ceramic King Cake baby or an uncooked dried bean
2 tablespoons water, for wash

Thaw puff pastry dough according to manufacturer's instructions on the package. Preheat oven to 450°F.

For the almond cream: In the bowl of an electric mixer fitted with a paddle attachment (or standard beater on a hand mixer at a slow speed), combine the almond paste, butter and granulated sugar. Slowly add the 4 eggs, one by one, until the filling is smooth. Scrape down the sides of the bowl between each egg addition. Add the flour and vanilla or rum extract to taste.

Take one sheet of the puff pastry dough and roll it out on a lightly floured surface into a 12-inch circle. Place on the floured, cutout disc. Roll a second sheet into an 11-inch circle.

Spread the almond cream in the center of the 12-inch pastry circle, leaving a 1-inch space from the edge. Place the King Cake baby or bean somewhere on the edge of the cream, if baking it in the cake. Place the  smaller 11-inch pastry circle on the top of the cream.

In a small bowl, lightly beat the remaining egg with the water and brush the exposed edge of the pastry with the egg wash. Fold the bottom edge over the top and pinch it to seal the cake. Now place the 11-inch disc on top of the pastry and gently flip the cake over, placing it on a baking sheet. Carefully slide the disc out from under the cake and remove the 12-inch disc from the top.

Brush the top with the egg wash and make a few decorative slashes in the pastry with a very sharp knife or razor blade.

Bake until the top is golden brown, about 12 to 15 minutes Reduce oven temperature to 375°F. Bake about 10 to 15 minutes more.

After the cake is cooled, top with a party-hat crown, and other Mardi Gras decorations, if desired, and serve. Whoever discovers the baby or bean is the king or queen!

—Recipe provided by Alain Levy, CIA Associate Professor—Baking and Pastry Arts. The Culinary Institute of America, 1996.

Take This Movement Further

BAKING BREAD IS something I never thought I'd do. And yet, it is one more step in making my life my own, understanding how I feel about things, what I believe, and how I want to live my life. When I was a new college graduate living in New York City and working at a trade newspaper, my life became frenetic. I took two buses to work every day and two buses back home to my apartment every night. If I wanted to exercise at a gym, I had to pack everything in a bag and lug it across town before or after work. There was a lot of frantic planning in post-graduate life in a big, big city. The only way I learned to relax was to come home at the end of the day, meet my roommate (who was a childhood friend), shed our work clothes in favor of comfortable attire, turn on mellow, lyric-less music and cook dinner.

In that small midtown apartment, I learned that you couldn't rush the process of making food. Everything has its set cooking time until it is edible, until it becomes what you have intended. As a naturally impatient person, I tended to rush through everything to get it done—but in the kitchen, I could not. Cooking forced me to breathe, to ponder, to *be*.

The busier my family life gets, the more important it is for us to make nourishing food from scratch. When we prepare to honor the weekly Sabbath, the most important preparation, then, is the making of the holy bread—to know that we can create our personal meaning from the work of our hands and not rely on anyone else to create the focus and the life that we want. That's the perspective from which this book was born—and it is the perspective I hope you will leave with: Go out into the world, and into your communities, and invite others to share in the process of making meaning from the mundane.

The very concept of holy breads is one that suggests that we can take simple ingredients—the basic foods that sustain us—and elevate them to something so much more. I encourage you to discover new rituals for your beliefs, new ways to create meaning in your midst and share them with us at www.TheFlavorsofFaith.com, and with me personally at www.LynneGolodner.com. Every day is another opportunity to find the flavor behind our faiths, and to share them with the world, so that we can stumble upon the universal truths that connect us all.

The very last thought I'd like to leave you with is the concept of connection as it relates to this book. There are no particular websites or books that are my favorites, but I love to explore, to discover, to wander. I have a conversation with every person I meet and sometimes I ask them to share their favorite resources with me. When you share in a meaningful experience with someone, ask them about their holy breads and then exchange favorite recipes. Let the foods of your faith be a point of connection with many others. The best thing we can do is to share these newfound discoveries with the world.

Making bread can seem daunting—but it only is if you let it be. My first meals were made in college—a box of pasta, a bottle of salad dressing, some parmesan cheese. And now, I try any recipe I stumble across. Some breads I've made turn out like doorstops. So we laugh and struggle through a few bites and feel completely comfortable tossing it in the garbage. But the more recipes you try, the better you'll get. Think of that sourdough loaf I told you about in the beginning of the book—the more weeks we made it, the lighter it got. Each loaf is better than the one before it because you slowly become expert in the art of bread making. Life is like that. You have to roll up your sleeves and feel the dough with your hands in order to know. You cannot become expert at anything from afar. And from a distance, nothing can enhance your knowledge of the Divine. Holiness is an intimate process and one that requires sensory experience. Dive in. You won't be sorry.

Acknowledgements

THIS HAS BEEN an exciting project for me since the idea first came together several years ago at a coffee shop table with my long-time friend, colleague and mentor David Crumm. We knew we wanted to work together on a book and the idea of bringing food and faith together was particularly enticing, given the ways in which we all use food to nourish, nurture and mark the meaningful moments of our lives. David's guidance and editing were stellar.

I'd like to acknowledge so many people who made this book happen, not the least of which are the generous individuals who gave me their time and attention, recipes and articles, and interviews over the phone, via email and in person. They include, but are not limited to, Annabel Cohen, Aviva Sandler, Fay Hamood, Nancy Makki, Imam Qazwini, Nephi Craig, Bill Tonelli, Jon Petrie, Andrea Slonecker, Maggie Glezer, Joe Lewis, Father Dan Merz, Carter Echols, Chef Alain Levy and Ginny Mure from the Culinary Institute of America, Arthur Hardy and Leonda

Levchuk at the National Museum of the American Indian. I want to thank so many other people who gave me their time and helped me get to the sources for this book. I want to also thank David Crumm, John Hile and the entire team at ReadtheSpirit Books for working with me on this project and making it possible.

Were it not for my lovely children, I would never have known the beauty of making bread from scratch. Thank you to Asher, Eliana and Shaya, for being wonderful sous-chefs and cooking companions, and of course expert tasters. You know well the peace of watching ingredients come together to form dough, the way the dough punches back when we knead it on the counter, the way it rises and grows and expands, like the possibility we always believe is in front of us, and the way it tastes when we sink our teeth into a homemade slice of bread, warm from the oven. It has made the ritual of our lives so much more special to do it over bread made from our very own hands.

My family has grown since I first began baking bread, so I must acknowledge the love and support of my entire family: my wonderful husband Dan, who defines me as writer above all else; all of my children: Asher, Eliana, Grace, and Shaya; and of course my extended family. I can still remember Grandpa Artie saying the Friday night blessing over bread and hiding the middle matzah under a pillow on his chair at Passover. It was at Grandma Sheila and Grandpa Artie's holiday and Sabbath tables that I learned to nourish the soul and the flame of tradition and heritage through food.

I want to remember my mentor and friend Jeff Zaslow, the esteemed book author and *Wall Street Journal* columnist whose life ended far too soon. At our last lunch, Jeff was incredibly enthusiastic about this book, believing in its power to connect people and communities. He was always an inspiration and a guiding force.

To all the editors who've given me work over the years and helped me hone my skills and my voice; my clients within my company, Your People LLC, for allowing me the freedom to work for myself and do creative side projects like this.

And of course I must thank the Source of everything, the God who lives in each one of us and guides our days and our decisions, loves us in the darkness of the night and in the brightness of the day.

About the Author

AFTER 15 YEARS as a journalist for national media in New York, Washington, D.C., and Detroit, Lynne Meredith Golodner created Your People LLC (www.yourppl.com) to provide marketing, public relations and business development for entrepreneurs, businesses and nonprofits. The Detroit-based business specializes in building business by building relationships. Lynne speaks extensively and frequently on business topics including marketing and public relations. An adjunct professor at University of Detroit Mercy, Lynne is a widely published author and guest speaker; this is her eighth book. Her book on Jewish women and hair covering, *Hide and Seek*, has gone through several printings and met with worldwide acclaim. She has two poetry books and

five non-fiction books published, including *Stand Out From the Crowd*, a DIY business book. Lynne lives in Southfield, Michigan with her husband, Dan, and their four children.

Colophon

READ THE SPIRIT Books produces its titles using innovative digital systems that serve the emerging wave of readers who want their books delivered in a wide range of formats—from traditional print to digital readers in many shapes and sizes. This book was produced using this entirely digital process that separates the core content of the book from details of final presentation, a process that increases the flexibility and accessibility of the book's text and images. At the same time, our system ensures a well-designed, easy-to-read experience on all reading platforms, built into the digital data file itself.

David Crumm Media has built a unique production workflow employing a number of XML (Extensible Markup Language) technologies. This workflow, allows us to create a single digital "book" data file that can be delivered quickly in all formats from traditionally bound print-on-paper to nearly any digital reader you care to choose, including Amazon Kindle®, Apple iBook®, Barnes and Noble Nook®

and other devices that support the ePub and PDF digital book formats.

And due to the efficient "print-on-demand" process we use for printed books, we invite you to visit us online to learn more about opportunities to order quantities of this book with the possibility of personalizing a "group read" for your organization or congregation by putting your organizations logo and name on the cover of the copies you order. You can even add your own introductory pages to this book for your church or organization.

During production, we use Adobe InDesign®, <Oxygen/>® XML Editor and Microsoft Word® along with custom tools built in-house.

The print edition is set in Minion Pro and Avenir Next fonts.

Cover art and Design by Rick Nease:www.RickNeaseArt.com.

Photography of baked goods by Stephanie Fenton.

Editing by David Crumm.

Copy editing and XML styling by Celeste Dykas and Dmitri Barvinok.

Digital encoding and print layout by John Hile.

If you enjoyed this book, you may also enjoy

FRIENDSHIP
FAITH

The WISDOM of women
creating alliances for peace

By the Women of WISDOM*

*Women's Interfaith Solutions for Dialogue and Outreach in MetroDetroit

Finding a good friend is hard. Preserving a friendship across religious and cultural boundaries—a challenge we all face in our rapidly changing world—is even harder.

http://www.FriendshipAndFaith.com

ISBN: 978-1-934879-19-1

If you enjoyed this book, you may also enjoy

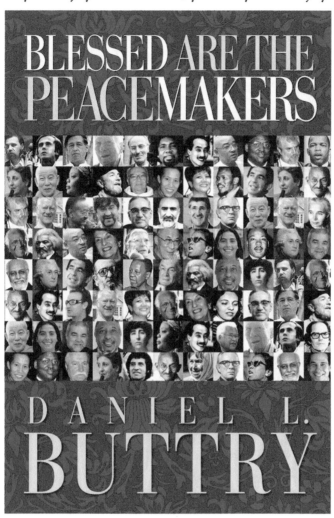

In the pages of this book, you will meet more than 100 heroes. Watch out! Reading about their lives may inspire you to step up into their courageous circle.

http://www.BlessedAreThePeacemakers.info

ISBN: 978-1-934879-76-4

If you enjoyed this book, you may also enjoy

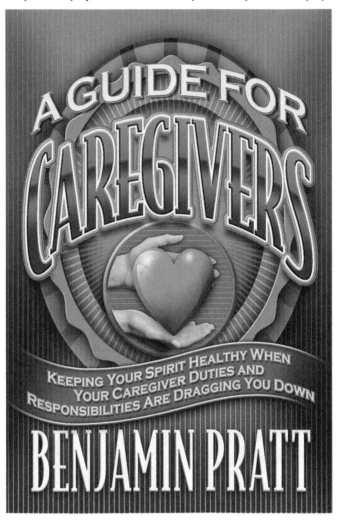

In one out of three households, someone is a caregiver: women and men who give of body, mind and soul to care for the well being of others. They need daily, practical help in reviving their spirits and avoiding burnout.

http://www.GuideForCaregivers.com

ISBN: 978-1-934879-27-6

If you enjoyed this book, you may also enjoy

In "This Jewish Life: Stories of Discover, Connection, and Joy", fifty-five voices enable readers to experience a calendar's worth of Judaism's strengths—community, healing, transformation of the human spirit and the influence of the Divine.

http://www.ThisJewishLife.com

ISBN: 978-1-934879-36-8

CPSIA information can be obtained at www.ICGtesting.com
Printed in the USA
BVOW11s2034210514

354153BV00012B/91/P